AMAZING TENNESSEE!

FALL IN LOVE WITH TENNESSEE THROUGH INTERESTING FUN FACTS AND TRIVIA FOR THE ENTIRE FAMILY

AMAZING STATES OF AMERICA

MARIANNE JENNINGS

KNOWLEDGE
NUGGET BOOKS

Copyright and Disclaimer

Amazing Tennessee!
Fall in Love with Tennessee through Interesting Fun Facts and Trivia for the Entire Family

Amazing States of America Series

Copyright © 2024 Knowledge Nugget Books
www.knowledgenuggetbooks.com
Willard, Utah & Liverpool, England

All rights reserved. No part of this publication may be reproduced, distributed, or transmitted in any form or by any means, including photocopying, recording, or other electronic or mechanical methods, without prior written permission of the publisher, except in the case of brief quotations embodied in reviews and certain other non-commercial uses permitted by copyright law.

For permissions contact: hello@knowledgenuggetbooks.com

Cover design by Paul Hawkins
Edited by Joe Levit
Fact-checked by Hank Musolf

Trademarks that are mentioned are done without written consent and can in no way be considered an endorsement from the trademark holder.

Library of Congress Control Number: 2024923558
ISBN 979-8-9884402-6-0 (paperback)
ISBN 979-8-9884402-7-7 (ebook)

Disclaimer:

Proceed with caution, Ya'll.

The author is not responsible for sudden urges to break into country tunes, spontaneous recitals of Civil War history, or uncontainable cravings for BBQ ribs.

Reading this book will not grant you the skills to rock the Grand Ole Opry, master the mysteries of the Great Smoky Mountains, or debate the virtues of whiskey versus moonshine.

While every attempt has been made to ensure the accuracy of this book, the author bears no responsibility for readers who decide to converse with bluegrass bands, argue with honky-tonk bouncers, or trace the spirited steps of Davy Crockett. Always remember: Tennessee's heart and soul resonate deeper than any page can capture!

ALSO BY MARIANNE JENNINGS

Entire Knowledge Nugget Book fun fact collection

So You Think You Know CANADA, Eh? (2nd Edition)

Amazing Tennessee!

Amazing Alaska!

Everything About Astronauts Vol 1 & 2

Quirky Careers & Offbeat Occupations

Christmas Fun Facts!

To the people of Tennessee and all who feel the pull of its mountains, music, and spirit—this book is a celebration of the stories and fun facts that make this state amazing and unforgettable.

HOW TO READ THIS BOOK

This book is divided into topics, making it easy to jump to any section you'd like.

There is no need to read this book cover to cover.

Just pick a subject that seems interesting and dig right in.

To test yourself and your friends with what you've learned, you'll find a fun, short quiz with answers in the back.

Bookmark All the Helpful Tennessee Resources

Find all of the fun and helpful Tennessee resources mentioned throughout this book (plus a few extras) including color images, videos, recipes, recommended Tennessee Books and more at:

KnowledgeNuggetBooks.com/resources

TABLE OF CONTENTS

Free Special Bonus	xiii
Introduction	xv

1. Essential Tennessee Tidbits — 1
2. Highs, Lows & Other Tennessee Geology Facts — 23
3. Crazy Tennessee Weather — 28
4. Tennessee's Wild & Rugged Nature — 32
5. Tennessee's Wildlife & Animal Facts — 49
6. Tennessee's Trees and Plants — 63
7. Tennessee's People & Population — 73
8. Tennessee Culture & Southern Hospitality — 80
9. Industry and Economy — 86
10. Tennessee & Sports — 92
11. Famous Inventions Made in Tennessee — 102
12. Random and Awesome — 111
13. You Know You're in Tennessee When... — 119
14. Fun Food and Drink Facts — 122
15. Interesting War History — 134
16. Tennessee's History of Slavery and Civil Rights — 146
17. Movies Filmed in Tennessee — 152
18. TV Shows filmed in Tennessee — 157
19. Famous Tennesseans — 160
20. Superstitions, Myths & Mysterious Creatures — 175
21. Famous Attractions & Unique Festivals — 179
22. Ways to See & Explore Tennessee — 197
23. Learn to Speak Tennessean — 213
24. Odd Tennessean Laws — 221
25. Quotables & Quirky Tennessee-isms — 224
26. Quiz Yourself — 229
27. Quiz Answers — 234

Acknowledgments	239
Don't Forget Your Free Special Bonus	241
Learn Something? Please Leave A Review	243
Want to Be a Beta Reader?	245
About the Author	247
Also by Marianne Jennings	249

FREE SPECIAL BONUS

As a **special bonus** and as a **thank you** for downloading this book, I created a **FREE companion quiz e-book** with **over 100 fun questions and answers** taken from this book.

Get the FREE bonus quiz e-book here:
https://tinyurl.com/tennessee-bonus

Test your knowledge of Tennessee and quiz your friends. Enjoy!

INTRODUCTION

When I think of Tennessee, I think of lively music scenes, mouth-watering BBQ, breathtaking mountain views, and the birthplace of rock 'n' roll and country music. This southern gem is a state bursting with culture, history and a vibrant spirit that's uniquely its own.

I've always been captivated by Tennessee's rich tapestry of Southern hospitality, traditions and innovations. To share my love for this amazing state, I've put together what I hope will be an engaging book packed with fun facts, intriguing tidbits and delightful stories.

Did you know Tennessee is home to the world's largest underground lake? Or that the Tennessee Renaissance Festival is the only one in the country that takes place at a real castle, the same one Taylor Swift made famous in one of her music videos? And let's not forget, Tennessee is where Mountain Dew and Mini-Golf were invented.

INTRODUCTION

In this book, we'll journey through the heart of Tennessee, uncovering its musical roots in Memphis and Nashville, where legends like Elvis Presley and Dolly Parton got their start. You'll learn about the mysterious Bell Witch of Adams, a ghost story that still sends shivers down spines. And we'll explore natural wonders like the Great Smoky Mountains, which is the most-visited national park in the country, and for good reason.

Through this book, I hope you'll enjoy some new knowledge, chuckle a bit and find a few fun nuggets to share with your friends. Whether you're a lifelong Tennessean or just curious about this charming state, prepare to be entertained and amazed by the captivating trivia that make Tennessee truly special.

So, get ready to dive into the wonders of Tennessee!

Please enjoy and stay curious!

Marianne

1

ESSENTIAL TENNESSEE TIDBITS

Map of Tennessee and where it is within the United States. Image via depositphotos.com

TENNESSEE'S NAME AND WHAT IT MEANS

The name "Tennessee" comes from the Cherokee word "Tanasi," associated with a village site called Tanasse, also spelled Tennese. The precise meaning of "Tanasi" remains unclear, though some suggest it might refer to the area near present-day Knoxville. The name has also been linked to the principal river running through the state, with some interpretations suggesting it means "bend in the river." However, this interpretation hasn't been proven, and the true meaning is considered lost.

The word "Tennessee" represents a rich blend of Native American heritage and European history, encapsulated in just one word, as it was officially adopted as the state's name in 1796.

TENNESSEE'S DISTINCTIVE NAME
The name "Tennessee" stands out for its memorable spelling and pronunciation, which also make it one of the most frequently misspelled state names. Common errors include "Tennesee," "Tennisse," "Tennissee," and "Tennisee."

These variations often result from omitting or rearranging letters, with the distinctive double 'n' and double 's' adding to the spelling challenge.

TENNESSEE'S NICKNAME
Tennessee is often referred to as the "Volunteer State." This nickname originated during the War of 1812 when Tennessee played a significant role in providing volunteers for the military.

SLOGAN ON LICENSE PLATES
Tennessee license plates have featured the state's nickname, "The Volunteer State," since the 1950s. It serves as a reminder of the state's proud history and the willingness of its residents to serve and contribute.

THE 16ᵀᴴ U.S. STATE
Tennessee officially became the 16th state of the United States on June 1, 1796. Prior to statehood, Tennessee was part of the Southwest Territory, which was established in 1790 and encompassed present-day Tennessee, Kentucky, Alabama, and Mississippi.

TENNESSEE'S CAPITAL
The state capital of Tennessee is Nashville. The city of Nashville was founded on Christmas Day in 1797. Known for its rich music heritage, especially in country music, Nashville is often referred to as "Music City, U.S.A."

The Tennessee State Capitol building is one of 12 state capitols that does not have a dome.

UNUSUAL STATE CAPITAL RULE
Tennessee is the only state that mandates its state capital (Nashville) to always remain the state capital. This law was written into the state constitution.

DID YOU KNOW?
During the American Civil War, Nashville was the first southern state capital to fall to Union troops. Its strategic location made it a prime target.

DAYLIGHT SAVINGS TIME
Tennessee participates in Daylight Savings Time, like the majority of the U.S. states, from March to November.

TIME ZONE SPLIT: A TALE OF TWO TIMES

Tennessee straddles two time zones. While most of the state—including major cities like Nashville and Memphis—follows Central Time, a portion of its eastern area, including Chattanooga, operates on Eastern Time. This division creates a one-hour time difference within the same state, a peculiarity that can be confusing for visitors traveling across Tennessee.

SHARES A BORDER WITH 8 OTHER STATES

Map of Tennessee showing surrounding states. Photo via depositphotos.com

The state of Tennessee and Missouri are tied when it comes to bordering the most other states. Tennessee shares a border with these eight states: Kentucky, Virginia, North Carolina, Georgia, Alabama, Mississippi, Arkansas and Missouri.

A TAPESTRY OF 95 COUNTIES

Tennessee is divided into 95 counties. This number has remained unchanged since 1919, when Pickett County was established as the last new county. Tennessee's counties vary significantly in size and population.

Shelby County, which includes the city of Memphis and its over 930,000 residents, is the most populous. Pickett County, known for its natural beauty, has the smallest population, with around 5,000 residents. In terms of area, Shelby County isn't the largest; that title goes to Cumberland County, covering the most land area in Tennessee.

TENNESSEE'S THREE GRAND DIVISIONS
Tennessee is famously divided into three Grand Divisions: East, Middle and West Tennessee. This division is not just geographical but also reflects cultural and historical differences. The state flag's three stars symbolize these divisions in a circle of unity.

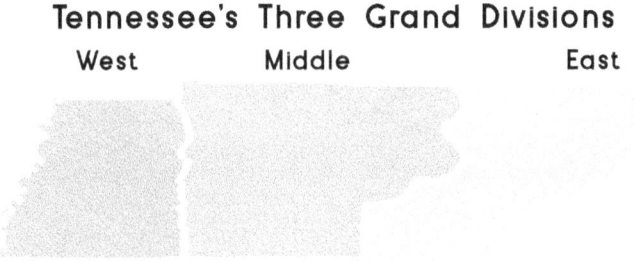

Tennessee's Three Grand Divisions. Map graphic created by the author

EAST TENNESSEE: THE MOUNTAINOUS LAND

- **Geographical Majesty:** East Tennessee is renowned for its breathtaking mountainous terrain, including the Great Smoky Mountains and the Appalachian Mountains. This region is a paradise for outdoor enthusiasts.
- **Birthplace of Country Music:** Bristol, in East Tennessee, is recognized as the "Birthplace of

Country Music," thanks to the 1927 Bristol Sessions, which had a significant impact on the country music genre.
- **Atomic History:** Oak Ridge, located in this division, played a pivotal role in the Manhattan Project during World War II. The city was developed as a secret site for uranium enrichment.
- **Cultural Richness:** East Tennessee is also known for its distinct Appalachian culture, which includes a variety of musical styles, crafts and storytelling traditions.

MIDDLE TENNESSEE: THE HEARTLAND

- **State Capital:** Middle Tennessee is home to Nashville, the state capital and the heart of the country music industry. The area is a hub for music, education and politics.
- **Lush Farmlands:** This division is characterized by fertile lands and rolling hills, making it a key agricultural area. It's known for its beautiful landscapes and charming small towns.
- **Historic Battlefields:** Middle Tennessee has a rich Civil War history, with significant battlefields like the Battle of Stones River and the Battle of Franklin. These sites are a window into the nation's past.
- **Educational Centers**: The region is known for its prestigious universities, including Vanderbilt University in Nashville and Middle Tennessee State University in Murfreesboro.

WEST TENNESSEE: THE LAND OF THE DELTA

- **The Mississippi Delta:** West Tennessee lies in the Mississippi Delta and is known for its rich, fertile soil, which supports a strong agricultural sector, particularly in cotton farming.
- **Musical Legacy:** Memphis, the largest city in this division, is a major cultural center with a deep musical heritage in blues, soul and rock 'n' roll. Iconic locations include Beale Street and Graceland, Elvis Presley's home.
- **Economic Hub:** West Tennessee serves as an economic hub, with Memphis playing a key role due to its status as a major transportation and logistics center.
- **Natural Wonders:** Reelfoot Lake in the northwest corner of Tennessee, created by a series of earthquakes in the early 19th century, is known for its fishing, eagle viewing and cypress forests.

STATE FLAG COMPETITION

In 1905, Tennessee sought to establish its own state flag, leading to a competition that captured the creative spirit of its residents.

Captain LeRoy Reeves, a member of the Tennessee National Guard, rose to the challenge with a design that resonated deeply with the state's values. His design, chosen for its simplicity and symbolism, was officially adopted on April 17, 1905, and has since become a proud emblem of Tennessee's heritage, unity and resilience.

The Tennessee state flag features a field of crimson red with a blue circle in the center. A vertical blue bar edged with white on the fly end of the flag provides a distinctive contrast and balance to the red background.

Tennessee State Flag. Image via depositphotos.com

- **The Three Stars:** Central to the flag's design are three white stars on a blue circle. These stars represent Tennessee's three Grand Divisions—East, Middle and West Tennessee. They are arranged in a circle to symbolize the harmony among these divisions. The circle's blue color reflects the state's commitment to unity and the richness of its cultural and natural landscapes.
- **Field of Red**: The majority of the flag's background is red, a color representing valor and the pioneering spirit of the state. This vibrant red field sets a bold and energetic backdrop for the central emblem.
- **The Vertical Blue Stripe**: The flag has a vertical blue stripe at the far right, a design element to add distinction when the flag is hanging limp. This stripe

was included to prevent the flag from looking like a solid red field when not flying in the wind.

TENNESSEE STATE SYMBOLS

Tennessee's state symbols are the Tulip Poplar (state tree), Iris (state flower), Tennessee River Pearl (state gem), Agate (state mineral), Limestone (state rock), Firefly, also known as the Lightning Bug (state insect), Honeybee (state agricultural insect), Eastern Box Turtle (state reptile), Zebra Swallowtail (state butterfly), Raccoon (state wild animal), Smallmouth Bass (state sport fish), Channel Catfish (state commercial fish) Northern Mockingbird (state bird), Tennessee Walking Horse (state horse), Rodeo (state sport), The Square Dance (state dance), Tomato (state fruit) and Milk (state beverage).

MORE THAN ONE OFFICIAL STATE SONG

Tennessee has 10 official state songs, including "The Tennessee Waltz," "Rocky Top," and "Tennessee," which reflect the state's strong musical traditions and cultural significance. Here are all official Tennessee State Songs:

"My Homeland, Tennessee" (1925): Tennessee's first official state song was adopted in 1925. Nell Grayson Taylor penned the lyrics and entered them into a contest seeking a patriotic anthem for Tennessee. Roy Lamont Smith added the music, and their collaboration won the competition, leading the Tennessee General Assembly to honor the song by making it the state's official anthem.

First Verse
O Tennessee, that gave us birth,
To thee our hearts bow down

For thee our love and loyalty
Shall weave a fadeless crown
Thy purple hills our cradle was;
Thy fields our mother breast
Beneath thy sunny bended skies,
Our childhood days were blessed

Second Verse
'Twas long ago our fathers came,
A free and noble band,
Across the mountain's frowning heights
To seek a promised land
And here before their raptured eyes;
In beauteous majesty:
Outspread the smiling valleys
Of the winding Tennessee

Third Verse
Could we forget our heritage
Of heroes strong and brave?
Could we do aught but cherish it,
Unsullied to the grave?
Ah no! the State where Jackson sleeps,
Shall ever peerless be
We glory in thy majesty;
Our homeland, Tennessee

Chorus
O Tennessee: Fair Tennessee:
Our love for thee can never die:
Dear homeland, Tennessee

"When It's Iris Time in Tennessee" (1935):

Written by Willa Waid Newman and adopted in 1935, this song celebrates Tennessee's state flower, the iris. The song was part of a campaign to promote the iris, which helped establish it as the state flower, replacing the passionflower.

First Verse
Sweetness of Spring memories bring
Of a place I long to be
Land of Sunshine calls this old heart of mine,
Come back to Tennessee

Second Verse
Rocks and the rills deep tinted hills,
There's no spot so dear to me
Where'er I roam still it's my Home Sweet Home,
My own, my Tennessee

Chorus
When it's Iris time down in Tennessee,
I'll be coming back to stay
Where the mockingbird sings at the break of day
A lilting love song gay
Where the Iris grows,
Where the Harpeth flows,
That is where I long to be
There's a picture there that lives in memory
When it's Iris time in Tennessee

"My Tennessee" (1955): Poet and songwriter Frances Hannah Tranum wrote "My Tennessee," which became Tennessee's third official state song in

1955. It expresses deep affection for the state's landscapes and people. Tranum wrote the song as an ode to her home state while she was living abroad, longing for Tennessee's familiar sights and sounds.

First Verse
Beloved state, oh state of mine,
In all the world I could not find,
Where God has strewn with lavish hand,
More natural beauty o'er the land
From ev'ry stream and valley green
His wond'rous art is ever seen
Ah, let my heart beat true to thee,
And swell with pride for Tennessee

Second Verse
Thy rocks and rills, and wooded hills,
My mem'ry keeps the childhood thrills
You gave to me, that I might know
The joys supreme, you could bestow
The song of birds, the whisp'ring trees,
The low of herds, the hum of bees,
It all comes back so dear to me,
My childhood home in Tennessee

Third Verse
Your battles fought, and vict'ries won,
Your freedom bought and duty done,
With daughters fair, and sons so brave,
To do and dare, their deeds they gave
Courageously, without a fear,
And won the name of volunteer
In sacred trust, let those who will,

By being just, preserve it still

Chorus
Oh, Tennessee, My Tennessee,
Thy hills and vales are fair to see,
With mountains grand, and fertile lands
There is no state more dear to me
Thro' other climes tho I may roam,
There will be times I'll long for home,
In Tennessee, Fair Tennessee,
The land of my nativity

"The Tennessee Waltz" (1965): Co-written by Redd Stewart and Pee Wee King on their way to Nashville. They were inspired by Bill Monroe's "Kentucky Waltz" and decided to come up with a version for Tennessee. "The Tennessee Waltz" was adopted as Tennessee's fourth official state song in 1965. Perhaps one of the most famous, this song has been a huge hit and has been recorded over 300 times in a variety of styles including rhythm and blues, pop, jazz, and rock.

I was waltzing with my darlin' to the Tennessee Waltz
When an old friend I happened to see
Introduced him to my loved one and while they were waltzing
My friend stole my sweetheart from me

I remember the night and the Tennessee Waltz
Now I know just how much I have lost
Yes I lost my little darlin' the night they were playing
The beautiful Tennessee Waltz

"Rocky Top" (1982): This lively bluegrass anthem was written by the husband-and-wife songwriting team, Felice and Boudleaux Bryant in just 10 minutes. "Rocky Top" is one of Tennessee's most famous and beloved songs. It became an official state song in 1982. If you've ever been to a University of Tennessee sporting event, you've definitely heard this one! The song is played so frequently at University of Tennessee events that it has become an unofficial fight song for the university.

First Verse
Wish that I was on ol' Rocky Top,
down in the Tennessee hills;
Ain't no smoggy smoke on Rocky Top;
Ain't no telephone bills;
Once I had a girl on Rocky Top;
Half bear, other half cat;
Wild as a mink, but sweet as soda pop,
I still dream about that;

Second Verse
Once two strangers climbed ol' Rocky Top,
lookin' for a moonshine still;
Strangers ain't come down from Rocky Top;
Reckon they never will;
Corn won't grow at all on Rocky Top;
Dirt's too rocky by far;
That's why all the folks on Rocky Top
get their corn from a jar;

Third Verse
I've had years of cramped-up city life

ESSENTIAL TENNESSEE TIDBITS

Trapped like a duck in a pen;
All I know is it's a pity life
Can't be simple again

Chorus
Rocky Top, you'll always be
home sweet home to me;
Good ol' Rocky Top;
Rocky Top, Tennessee;
Rocky Top, Tennessee

"Tennessee" (1992): Written by Vivian Rorie, "Tennessee" became an official state song in 1992. The song celebrates the spirit and beauty of Tennessee. Rorie composed this song as a tribute to her father and his deep love for Tennessee.

I do not know of another state
Where I had rather be
Than this great state I'm living in
And that is Tennessee.

I love the stars dearly
And there are surely three
That show the Grand Division
Of my home-land, Tennessee.

Where could you find a meadow
With grass so vividly green?
Where could you find the mountains
With such majestic scene?

You will never find so bright a moon

> To shine down from above
> You will also see the robin
> The wren, and the turtle dove.
>
> And don't forget the rivers
> Where visitors long to stay.
> And many have voice in parting,
> 'I'm sure glad I passed this way.'
>
> You will see the cattle grazing
> Beside a cotton field;
> And there's the Grand Ole Opry
> And a feeling it's all God's will.
>
> I have lived here all my life
> It's where I'm going to be
> Although I've traveled quite a bit,
> I'll still take Tennessee!
>
> Oh, I sure love the state I'm in:
> The great state of Tennessee!"

"The Pride of Tennessee" (1996): Written by Fred Congdon, Thomas Vaughn and Carol Elliot, this song was adopted as the state's official song in 1996. This song is a history lesson that shares details about 11 famous people featured in Tennessee's official Bicentennial painting. The song was performed at the 1996 Summer Olympics in Atlanta.

> From the Smokie Mountain Mornings to the
> Mississippi shores

Let's take time to remember those who went before
Whose lives made a difference in the world for you and me
Their courage faith and vision are the Pride of Tennessee
Sequoyah was a Cherokee the chief of all his tribe
His people learned to read and write with the alphabet he scribed
When Tennessee became a State its Governor was clear
There was no better leader than the gallant John Sevier
From the backwoods to the Congress to his stand at the Alamo
Davy Crockett gave his life for the country he loved so

Three Presidents from Tennessee made impressions on this land
Jackson, Polk and Johnson were men who took a stand
Ida Wells Barnett fought bravely for the rights of men
When they were killed by prejudice for the color of their skin
He was drafted in the first world war though he did not want to go
His shooting skills made Alvin York a national hero

*When women of Tennessee believed they had
   the right to vote
Ann Dallas Dudley led the fight and gave
   them hope
Cordell Hull had a vision for peace around the
   world
The United Nations where all countries' flags
   unfurl
From Beale Street down in Memphis to New
   York front page news
WC Handy's music made him father of the
   blues*

*Yes Courage, Faith and Vision are the Pride of
   Tennessee*

"Tennessee Bicentennial Rap" (1996):
Adopted in 1996, this unique rap by poet Joan Hill Hanks commemorates Tennessee's 200th anniversary with historical references and modern rhythm. Hanks wrote it originally as a poem as a fun and interesting way to teach students and citizens about the history of Tennessee.

*TENNE-, TENNE-, TENNES-SEE!
Oh, how proud we are of thee!
Volunteer State since 1812 —
Glad our fathers picked here to dwell!*

*Presidents, Presidents - proud are we!
Jackson, Polk, and Johnson - three!
Crockett, Forrest, and John Sevier;
Alvin York and Hull lived here!*

Baker, Gores, and Kefauver,
Served our country with honor!
U.T., Memphis and Vandy U.,
Tennessee Tech and Sewanee, too!

Appalachian Mountains, mountains high —
Reaching up in the smoky sky!
Tennessee River, flowing through —
We will cross near the Choo Choo!

Dollywood and Walking Horse Show!
Opryland and the Opry Show!
Whisky, whisky - sipping smooth —
Moon, Moon Pies and Goo Goo Goos!

Reelfoot Lake and cotton fields,
Natchez Trace and Civil War fields!
Mocking birds and raccoons grow,
And tulip poplars and iris show!

Bessie Smith and Memphis blues —
W.C. Handy and Elvis, too!
Eastman, Oak Ridge, and TVA —
Nissan, Saturn, and Country Music pay!

Chickasaw, Sequoyah, and Cherokee —
Cumberland Plateau and Mississippi!
BIRTHDAY WISHES ON 200 YEARS —
GIVE TENNESSEE A BIG, BIG CHEER!

"Smoky Mountain Rain" 2010: Written by Kye Fleming and Dennis Morgan and recorded by country music artist Ronnie Milsap, "Smoky Mountain Rain" was designated as Tennessee's official state popular song in 2010.

> I thumbed my way from LA back to Knoxville
> I found out those bright lights ain't where I
>   belong
> From a phone booth in the rain I called to
>   tell her
> I've had a change of dreams I'm comin' home
> But tears filled my eyes when I found out she
>   was gone
>
> Smoky Mountain rain keeps on fallin'
> I keep on callin' her name
> Smoky Mountain rain I'll keep on searchin'
> I can't go on hurtin' this way
> She's somewhere in the Smoky Mountain rain
>
> I waved a diesel down outside a cafe'
> He said that he was goin' as far as Gatlinburg
> I climbed up in the cab all wet and cold and
>   lonely
> I wiped my eyes and told him about her
> I've got to find her!
> Can you make these big wheels burn?
>
> Smoky Mountain rain keeps on fallin'
> I keep on callin' her name
> Smoky Mountain rain I'll keep on searchin'
> I can't go on hurtin' this way
> She's somewhere in the Smoky Mountain rain
>
> I can't blame her for lettin' go

A woman needs someone warm to hold
I feel the rain runnin' down my face
I'll find her no matter what it takes!

Smoky Mountain rain keeps on fallin'
I keep on callin' her name
Smoky Mountain rain I'll keep on searchin'
I can't go on hurtin' this way
She's somewhere in the Smoky Mountain rain

"Tennessee" (2012): Adopted in 2012, John R. Bean's "Tennessee" highlights the state's diverse landscapes and cultural legacy. Bean was inspired to write the song after a road trip across Tennessee, during which he absorbed local music and stories from different communities.

Oh Tennessee, I long to come back home.
I guess your dew has settled on my soul.
Everyday I stayed away,
You called my heart back, home to stay.
Oh Tennessee, I long to come back home.

Oh Tennessee, I'm missing you too soon.
Silver skies and lazy afternoons...
Silver clouds and golden moon,
You're Mother Nature's Tender Womb...
Oh Tennessee, I'm missing you too soon.

Your days, have such gentle ways
Aimless thoughts and windblown rhymes
Your nights sing such peaceful songs.
To a tired and weary mind.

Oh Tennessee, I've spent more than I've earned,
But I'm much richer now for what I've learned...
Money won't buy peace of mind,
And peace of mind is what I'll find...
Oh Tennessee, you treated me so kind.

DID YOU KNOW?

Three of Tennessee's 10 Official State Songs have been major hits. These are:
"Tennessee Waltz", "Rocky Top," and "Smoky Mountain Rain."

2

HIGHS, LOWS & OTHER TENNESSEE GEOLOGY FACTS

THE SIZE OF TENNESSEE

Tennessee covers an area of about 42,143 square miles (109,247 square kilometers). In terms of size, Tennessee is similar to Virginia, which has an area of approximately 42,775 square miles (110,787 square kilometers). Both states are mid-sized among the 50 U.S. states. Tennessee is the 36th largest state by area in the U.S.

Tennessee can be compared in size to the country Cuba, which has an area of about 42,426 square miles (109,884 square kilometers).

EAST-TO-WEST

From east to west, Tennessee is exactly 440 miles (708 km) wide! To put Tennessee's length in perspective, it's slightly longer than the distance between Los Angeles and San Francisco (around 380 miles or 611.5 km) and a bit shorter than the distance between Washington D.C. and Boston (around 460 miles or 740 km).

NORTH-TO-SOUTH

Tennessee is approximately 110 miles (177 kilometers) high from its northern border to its southern border. This measurement can vary slightly depending on the specific location, as the state's borders are not perfectly straight lines. To put that into perspective, 110 miles (177 km) is roughly the distance from New York City to Philadelphia.

TENNESSEE'S THREE REGIONS

Tennessee's charm is found in its harmonious trio of regions, known as the Grand Divisions: East, Middle and West Tennessee. Each region brings its own history, culture, and landscape, forming the heart and soul of the state.

EAST TENNESSEE

To the east, where the Appalachian Mountains rise majestically, lies East Tennessee. This region is a canvas painted by Mother Nature herself, featuring rolling hills, scenic vistas, and vibrant cities like Knoxville, Chattanooga, and Johnson City.

East Tennessee is home to the Great Smoky Mountains National Park, the most visited national park in the U.S. Its breathtaking peaks, diverse wildlife, and extensive trails make it a true gem of the region.

MIDDLE TENNESSEE

In the center of the state, Middle Tennessee bridges the mountainous east and the flat western plains. This area is characterized by lush farmland and gentle hills, with Nashville—the state capital and a cultural epicenter—at its heart. Nearby cities like Murfreesboro and Franklin add to the region's charm.

Middle Tennessee is often called the "Athens of the South" due to its prestigious educational institutions like Vanderbilt and Belmont University, making it a hub for intellectual and artistic pursuits.

WEST TENNESSEE
In the west, the land flattens out and becomes rich and fertile, influenced by the mighty Mississippi River. West Tennessee has a strong farming heritage, historically dominated by cotton. Memphis, Jackson, and Dyersburg are key cities here.

Memphis, the largest city in West Tennessee, is celebrated as the birthplace of Rock 'n' Roll and a cornerstone of the Blues. Iconic Beale Street and Elvis Presley's Graceland are just a few of its legendary attractions.

TALLEST POINT OF TENNESSEE
Perched gracefully along the state border of both Tennessee and North Carolina in the Great Smoky Mountains National Park is Clingmans Dome, standing tall as the Tennessee's highest peak. With an impressive elevation of 6,643 feet (2,025 meters), it doesn't just reign supreme in Tennessee but also holds the title of the highest point along the entire Appalachian Trail.

Visitors to Clingmans Dome are treated to a panoramic spectacle of the Smoky Mountains, with views that can span over 100 miles (161 km) on clear days. An observation tower at the summit further enhances this breathtaking experience.

What makes this spot even more enchanting is the blanket of

cool, misty fog that often envelops it, giving the Great Smoky Mountains their iconic name. Whether you're an avid hiker or just someone in search of majestic views, Clingmans Dome is a Tennessee treasure not to be missed.

A DOME OF MANY NAMES

Before being named Clingmans Dome, this high peak was referred to by many names, including "Smoky Dome" and "Red Knob." It's original name in Cherokee is Kuwahi or Kuwohi, which means "mulberry place."

HALF & HALF

While the observation tower of Clingmans Dome is a popular destination in the Great Smoky Mountains National Park, what many don't know is that the state line between North Carolina and Tennessee runs right through the dome. So, technically, you can stand in two states at once!

LOWEST POINT OF TENNESSEE

The lowest point in Tennessee—at about 178 feet (54 meters) above sea level—is located where the Mississippi River exits the state.

LOOKOUT MOUNTAIN – NOT THE HIGHEST, BUT SEVEN STATES CAN BE SEEN FROM THE SUMMIT

Lookout Mountain, straddling the border between Tennessee and Georgia, is a spectacular natural landmark offering breathtaking vistas and rich history. Though it isn't Tennessee's highest mountain, on a clear day visitors can enjoy the experience of seeing seven states from the summit. These states include: Alabama, Tennessee, North Carolina, South Carolina,

Georgia, Kentucky, and Virginia. There is even a glimpse of the Great Smoky Mountains National Park itself.

The mountain is steeped in Civil War history, notably the "Battle Above the Clouds" fought in 1863. Lookout Mountain also boasts the enchanting Rock City Gardens, with its ancient rock formations and the legendary "Lover's Leap," where according to legend, a Native American couple jumped to their deaths.

Additionally, the Incline Railway, called "America's Most Amazing Mile" is one of the steepest passenger railways in the world, offers a thrilling ride to the top of Lookout Mountain with a 72.7% grade on the approximately one-mile (1.6 km)-long single track.

Marker at the top of Lookout Mountain. Photo by Brent Moore, CC BY 2.0, via Wikimedia Commons

3

CRAZY TENNESSEE WEATHER

TENNESSEE'S FOUR SEASONS
Tennessee experiences all four distinct seasons, with each one offering a different and picturesque landscape. From the lush greenery of summer to the colorful foliage of autumn, the snow-covered winters, and the blossoming beauty of spring, the state truly enjoys the full spectrum of seasons for residents and visitors to enjoy.

TENNESSEE'S AVERAGE TEMPERATURES
Tennessee enjoys a varied climate with mild winters and warm summers. The average annual temperature is about 60°F (15.6°C). Western Tennessee, including Memphis, sees summer highs around 91°F (32.8°C) and winter lows around 34°F (1.1°C). In contrast, the eastern mountainous regions have cooler averages, with summer highs around 79°F (26.1°C) and winter lows around 23°F (-5°C). This range makes Tennessee a state of pleasant seasons and occasional extremes.

WHEN IT RAINS, IT POURS…ESPECIALLY IN THE MOUNTAINS

Some parts of Tennessee get quite a bit of rain. Tennessee is the sixth-rainiest U.S. state, with an average of 139 days of rain and 54.6 inches a year. The mountainous eastern border of the state including Mt. Le Conte and the Great Smoky Mountains are the rainiest parts of Tennessee, receiving an average of 73.5 inches of rain each year. To compare, the wettest city in the U.S. is Hilo, Hawaii, which receives 211 days of rain each year, on average.

LIGHTNING STRIKES

Tennessee ranks high in the nation for lightning strikes, with an average of around 819,000 cloud-to-ground flashes per year. This makes outdoor activities during thunderstorms particularly risky. Remember, "When thunder roars, go indoors!"

FLOODS OF 2010

In May 2010, Tennessee experienced a catastrophic flood, particularly in the Nashville area. Over 13 inches of rain fell in just two days, causing the Cumberland River to crest at 51.86 feet (15.8 meters), flooding the city. The damage was extensive, with losses estimated at over $2 billion. This made the flood one of the most severe weather events in the state's history.

DROUGHT DILEMMAS

Tennessee isn't immune to droughts either. One of the most significant droughts occurred in 2007, severely affecting agriculture and water supplies. The drought led to water restrictions in many communities and had a lasting impact on the state's economy.

HAILSTORMS AND HAILSTONES

While not as common as thunderstorms or tornadoes, hailstorms do occur in Tennessee. The largest recorded hailstone in Tennessee fell in Clarksville on May 18, 1995. It measured a whopping 4.5 inches in diameter—about the size of a grapefruit!

ICE STORMS

Ice storms are a significant winter hazard in Tennessee, often causing widespread damage and power outages. One of the most severe ice storms occurred in January 1994, affecting much of the state. The ice accumulation reached up to three inches in some areas, leading to massive power outages, dangerous travel conditions and significant tree damage. This storm did an estimated $3 billion in damage, becoming one of the costliest natural disasters in Tennessee history.

SNOW IN THE SOUTH?

While Tennessee isn't typically known for heavy snowfall, the state does get its fair share, especially in the eastern mountainous regions. The snowiest winter on record was the winter of 1959-1960, when parts of Tennessee received over 40 inches of snow. Nashville, on the other hand, averages about 6.3 inches of snow per year.

THE GREAT BLIZZARD OF 1993

Also known as the "Storm of the Century," the blizzard of March 1993 was one of the most severe winter storms to hit Tennessee. The storm dumped up to 20 inches (50.8 cm) of snow in parts of the state and brought below freezing temperatures. In some areas of the Great Smoky Mountains, there were reports of 56 inches (142 cm) of snow with drifts of 10-15 feet

(3-4.5 meters). This blizzard paralyzed much of the state for days, making it a memorable weather event for many residents.

TENNESSEE'S COLDEST DAY
Tennessee's coldest day ever happened on December 30, 1917 when it reached -32°F (-36°C) in Mountain City.

TENNESSEE'S HOTTEST DAY
The highest temperature ever recorded in Tennessee was 113°F (45°C) in Perryville on July 29, 1930.

SUMMER SIZZLE
Tennessee summers can be quite toasty! The combination of high temperatures and humidity often makes it feel even hotter, creating what's known as the "heat index."

FOGGY BOTTOMS
Tennessee's geography and river valleys contribute to frequent fog formation, particularly in the fall and winter months. The Tennessee River Valley is especially prone to dense fog, which can reduce visibility and make driving hazardous. This is a lesser-known weather characteristic that impacts daily life for many Tennesseans.

THE TORNADO TANGO
Did you know that Tennessee is a part of "Dixie Alley," an area in the southern United States known for its high frequency of tornadoes? On average, Tennessee experiences about 29 tornadoes per year. One of the most notable tornado outbreaks occurred in April 2011, when several tornadoes hit the state in a single day, causing significant damage.

4

TENNESSEE'S WILD & RUGGED NATURE

THE GREAT SMOKY MOUNTAINS

The Great Smoky Mountains, straddling the border between Tennessee and North Carolina, are renowned for their stunning natural beauty and rich biodiversity. As part of the Appalachian Mountain chain, they are home to the Great Smoky Mountains National Park, the most visited national park in the United States, with over 12 million visitors annually.

ANCIENT MOUNTAINS

The Great Smoky Mountains are among the oldest mountains in the world, formed some 200-300 million years ago during the Paleozoic Era. They are a subrange of the Appalachian Mountains, which are thought to have formed as a result of the collision of the North American and African tectonic plates.

WHY ARE THEY CALLED THE SMOKY MOUNTAINS?

Low clouds covering the mountain tops in the Great Smoky Mountain National Park. Photo by adogslifephoto via depositphotos.com

The Great Smoky Mountains get their name from the natural fog that often covers them, creating a mystical, smoke-like effect. This fog isn't actual smoke, though. It happens because the trees and plants in the area release chemicals into the air.

These chemicals interact with sunlight, causing a bluish haze to form, especially in the morning and evening. This gives the mountains their famous "smoky" appearance.

The Cherokee people, who originally inhabited the region, called these mountains "Shaconage," meaning "place of the blue smoke," reflecting the same phenomenon.

NATIONAL PARK

BIO-DIVERSITY HAVEN
The Great Smoky Mountains National Park is a UNESCO World Heritage Site and an International Biosphere Reserve. It hosts over 19,000 documented species, but scientists believe there could be an additional 80,000 to 100,000 species yet to be discovered.

HISTORICAL SIGNIFICANCE
Before becoming a national park in 1934, the area was home to early settlers and indigenous Cherokee tribes. Numerous structures, like log cabins, barns, churches and grist mills have been preserved and can be visited today.

CADES COVE
Cades Cove is one of the most visited parts of the park, offering visitors a glimpse into 19th-century Appalachian life. This valley was once a hunting ground for the Cherokee before the European settlers arrived in the early 1800s.

DIVERSE WEATHER PATTERNS
The Smokies' topography creates varied weather

patterns, with higher elevations experiencing conditions similar to those found in Canada, while lower elevations are more temperate.

56 TENNESSEE STATE PARKS

Tennessee boasts 56 state parks, each offering its own slice of natural beauty and recreational opportunities. From the towering waterfalls of Fall Creek Falls State Park to the serene lakes of Tims Ford State Park, there's something for everyone. History buffs can explore significant sites like the Battle of Shiloh at Shiloh National Military Park, while adventure seekers can hike the rugged trails of South Cumberland State Park.

THE CUMBERLAND PLATEAU

The Cumberland Plateau stretches across Tennessee, offering stunning vistas, deep gorges, and distinctive rock formations. This plateau is one of the world's most biologically diverse areas, home to a variety of plants and animals, including some species found nowhere else on Earth. This includes the Cumberland Plateau Salamander, the Green Salamander, Cumberland Sandwort and the Southern Cave Crayfish.

MIGHTY MISSISSIPPI RIVER

Tennessee's western border is defined by the mighty Mississippi River. This river is not only a crucial waterway for commerce and transportation but also supports a rich ecosystem. The river's floodplain provides habitat for numerous wildlife species and is a vital migration route for birds.

Tennessee Tops the Cave Charts!

CAVES AND CAVERNS

With over 10,000 documented caves and caverns, Tennessee has more caves than any other U.S. state. The majority of these caves can be found in the Cumberland Plateau region. The limestone bedrock in the Cumberland Plateau is easily dissolved by water, which is why there are so many caves in this region. The caves range in size from small, one-room caves to large, complex cave systems.

Some of the most famous caves in Tennessee include:

NICKAJACK BAT CAVE

Nickajack Bat Cave, nestled near Nickajack Lake in Marion County, Tennessee, is a bat-lover's paradise. Nickajack Cave is home to a large population of endangered gray bats. During the summer months, up to 100,000 bats roost in the cave, making it one of the most important bat habitats in the southeastern United States. The Tennessee Wildlife Resources Agency (TWRA) designated the cave as the state's first non-game wildlife refuge in 1992 to protect these bats.

One of the best ways to experience the cave is by taking a guided kayak tour at sunset. These tours offer a front-row seat to witness thousands of bats emerging from the cave to hunt for insects.

Nickajack Cave has been a known landmark for hundreds of years, serving various purposes throughout history. It was first a shelter for Native Americans, and then later used by river pirates. The cave was also a significant source of saltpeter, a key ingredient in gunpowder, during the War of 1812 and the Civil War.

RUBY FALLS

Ruby Falls within a cave in Tennessee. Photo by sergey.miami2you.com via depositphotos.com

Located within Lookout Mountain near Chattanooga, Ruby Falls is one of the most visited cave attractions in the U.S. It's America's deepest commercial cave, and the largest underground waterfall accessible to the public. The waterfall is situated more than 1,100 feet (335 meters) below the surface.

Ruby Falls was discovered accidentally in 1928 by cave enthusiast Leo Lambert. While drilling an elevator shaft to access Lookout Mountain Cave, Lambert and his team hit a void that led them to the previously unknown waterfall, which he named after his wife, Ruby, who played a pivotal role in the cave's exploration.

The waterfall plunges 145 feet (44 meters) into a cavernous pit, creating a mesmerizing spectacle that is beautifully illuminated for visitors.

During World War II, the cave system served as a secure storage site for important documents, including those of the Hamilton County Courthouse.

During the Cold War, Ruby Falls Cave was designated as a Civil Defense fallout shelter. It was stocked with supplies to sustain 720 people for several weeks, making it a safe place in the event of a nuclear attack.

Additionally, Ruby Falls was once home to a unique subterranean radio station, broadcasting country music deep from within the cave.

TUCKALEECHEE CAVERNS
Situated in Townsend, these caverns are known as the "Greatest Site Under the Smokies." They're home to the "Big Room," which is over 450 feet (137 meters) wide, and could almost fit an American football field, and Silver Falls, a beautiful and spectacular two-tiered underground waterfall that plunges 210 feet (64 meters), making it the tallest subterranean waterfall in the Eastern United States.

RACCOON MOUNTAIN CAVERNS
Initially discovered in 1929 by Leo Lambert, who also discovered Ruby Falls, the caverns were originally named the Tennessee Caverns and then changed to Crystal City Caves. Eventually, the name was changed to Raccoon Mountain Caverns in the late 1970s. The cave system has over 5.5 miles

(8.85 km) of explored and mapped passageways, with new discoveries still being made today.

Located just outside Chattanooga, Raccoon Mountain Caverns has an incredible array of formations, including stalactites, stalagmites, flowstone, soda straws, rimstone dams, and more. Due to the cleanliness and clarity of these formations, the cave often seems to sparkle from every angle.

The caverns are home to a variety of wildlife, including several species of salamanders and the unique Crystal Caverns Cave Spider (Nesticus furtivus), which is known to exist only within this cave system.

BELL WITCH CAVE

The Bell Witch Cave, located in Adams, Tennessee, is a significant site tied to the famous Bell Witch legend. This cave, formed through the gradual erosion of limestone by water (a process known as karst formation), spans approximately 490 feet (149 meters) and was discovered near the Bell family homestead. While the cave wasn't part of the original hauntings, it has since become central to the folklore surrounding the Bell Witch.

Today, the cave serves as a tourist attraction, offering guided tours where visitors can learn about the eerie history and explore artifacts from the Bell family era, including a reconstructed John Bell cabin. The cave is known for its mysterious tales, including the supposed rescue of a child by the witch, adding to its allure as one of America's most haunted locations.

CUMBERLAND CAVERNS

Situated in McMinnville, Cumberland Caverns is Tennessee's largest show cave and a U.S. National Natural Landmark. The Volcano Room within Cumberland Caverns is renowned for its near-perfect acoustics and has hosted numerous live music events, including the famous PBS series "Bluegrass Underground." An antique 8-by-15-foot (281.9 cm) crystal chandelier hangs from the ceiling in the Volcano Room.

Chandelier in the Volcano Room of the Cumberland Caverns. Photo by RL0919, CC BY-SA 4.0, via Wikimedia Commons

One of the most intriguing features is the "Neverending

Waterfall" within the caverns. Despite numerous dye tests conducted by researchers to trace the source and destination of the water, the origins remain a mystery. This waterfall, with its unique parachute formation, is a highlight of the cave tours.

A portion of the Trail of Tears passes through the property of Cumberland Caverns. There is a public walking trail that allows visitors to explore this historic route.

CRAIGHEAD CAVERNS
Craighead Caverns, located between Sweetwater and Madisonville, Tennessee, is home to the famous Lost Sea, the largest underground lake in the United States.

The caverns also showcase a variety of interesting geological formations, including anthodites (also known as "cave flowers"), stalactites, and stalagmites. These formations make the cave a geological treasure.

The Craighead Caverns get their name after a Cherokee chief called Chief Craighead. The caverns were used by the Cherokee for council meetings and other activities. Artifacts such as pottery, arrowheads, and jewelry have been found in a section of the cave known as the "Council Room."

During the Civil War, Confederate soldiers mined the cave for saltpeter, a key ingredient in gunpowder.

TENNESSEE SINKHOLES
Tennessee has over 54,000 sinkholes, which are large holes that suddenly appear when the ground collapses. These sinkholes form when water dissolves the limestone rock beneath the surface, creating underground spaces that eventually cave in.

Tennessee has lots of limestone, especially in the central and eastern parts, making it a hotspot for sinkholes.

The deepest sinkhole in Tennessee is called Big Sink in White County and is 262.7 feet (80 meters) deep. The biggest sinkhole in Tennessee with the biggest area and largest volume is Grassy Cove, at 5 square miles (12.9 square kilometers) and 131.1 feet (39.97 meters) deep.

DID YOU KNOW?
In Tennessee, insurance companies are legally required to offer sinkhole coverage to both businesses and homeowners.

LAND OF LAKES
Tennessee has approximately 1,000 lakes or man-made reservoirs, which are spread throughout the state. These bodies of water provide opportunities for boating, fishing and water sports. Kentucky Lake and Lake Barkley, two of the largest man-made lakes in the United States, offer thousands of miles of shoreline and are popular recreational destinations.

REELFOOT LAKE
Reelfoot Lake, located in the northwest corner of Tennessee, is a natural wonder created by the violent New Madrid earthquakes of 1811-1812, which caused the Mississippi River to flow backward and flood the area, forming the lake. Known for its cypress swamps and stunning sunsets, Reelfoot Lake is a haven for wildlife enthusiasts and bird watchers, especially during the winter months when bald eagles flock to the area.

The lake's shallow waters and rich biodiversity support a variety of fish, making it a popular fishing spot.

Reelfoot Lake is named after a legendary Chickasaw chief. According to local folklore, Chief Reelfoot had a physical deformity, giving him a twisted or "reelfoot." The legend says that he fell in love with a beautiful maiden from another tribe and kidnapped her against the wishes of her father and the Great Spirit. In response, the Great Spirit caused the earth to shake violently, creating the deep chasms and flooding that formed Reelfoot Lake. This dramatic and romantic legend adds a mystical aura to the lake's already fascinating geological origins.

THE LOST SEA, THE LARGEST UNDERGROUND LAKE IN THE UNITED STATES

Sweetwater, Tennessee, is home to The Lost Sea. America's largest underground lake is nestled within Craighead Caverns, and was discovered in 1905 by a 13-year-old boy named Ben Sands. As the story goes, Ben wriggled through a small muddy opening 300 feet (91.4 meters) underground and found himself in the large chamber housing the lake.

The visible part of the lake measures about 800 feet (243.8 meters) long and 220 feet (67 meters) wide. However, explorations have revealed that the entirety of the lake could span over 13 acres (5.26 hectares), with many sections yet to be mapped.

Visitors can marvel at stunning geological formations, including one of the world's largest stalagmites, and embark on a mesmerizing boat tour across the lake's dark waters.

The lake is home to a species of blind, pinkish rainbow trout. These fish have adapted to the dark environment, and their presence in the lake remains somewhat of a mystery.

LAND OF WATERFALLS

Tennessee boasts over 500 waterfalls, many of them hidden away in its vast wilderness areas. The Great Smoky Mountains are home to over 100 waterfalls (mostly above ground). The tallest waterfall in the park is Rainbow Falls, with a highest single-drop of 80 feet (24 meters).

FALL CREEK FALLS

Fall Creek Falls is located in Fall Creek Falls State Park within the Cumberland Plateau. At 256 feet (78 meters), it is one of the highest waterfalls in the eastern United States.

BIODIVERSITY HOTSPOT

Tennessee is a biodiversity hotspot, particularly within its numerous state parks and natural areas. The state is home to over 340 species of birds, 77 species of mammals, 315 species of fish, 56 species of reptiles, and 70 species of amphibians. The diverse habitats, ranging from wetlands to forests, contribute to this rich variety of wildlife.

HIDDEN ARCHES AND NATURAL BRIDGES

Tennessee is home to several natural rock arches and bridges. They are less well-known than those found in the western United States, but equally impressive.

> **Twin Arches:** Located in the Big South Fork National River and Recreation Area, the Twin

Arches are the largest natural bridge complex in Tennessee and among the largest in the world. The South Arch stands 103 feet (31 meters) tall and spans 135 feet (41 meters), while the North Arch is 62 feet (18.8 meters) high with a 93-foot (28 meter) span.

Sewanee Natural Bridge: The Natural Bridge in Sewanee is a stunning limestone arch that spans nearly 50 feet (15.2 meters) and was formed from a giant sinkhole that partially eroded.

Picket State Park: This park features several natural arches, including the impressive Natural Bridge. The easy mile-long (1.6 km) trail to the bridge passes through a hardwood forest and ends at the sandstone formation, which spans 86 feet (26 meters) in length and stands 35 feet (10.6 meters) high.

THE APPALACHIAN TRAIL

The Appalachian Trail, a famous hiking route stretching over 2,190 miles (3,524.4 km) from Georgia to Maine, passes through Tennessee. Hikers traversing the Tennessee section of the trail will experience some of the most rugged and scenic landscapes, including the Roan Highlands, known for their breathtaking views and vibrant wildflower displays.

The Tennessee section of the trail is approximately 287.9 miles (463.3 km) long, including the section along the Tennessee-North Carolina border. That section features some of the highest elevations on the entire trail, such as Clingmans Dome at 6,643 feet (2,024.7 meters). The trail offers diverse terrain, from the lush forests and wildflower-covered tops of the Roan

Highlands to challenging ascents in the Great Smoky Mountains National Park.

Notably, the trail through Tennessee is known for its "balds," which are treeless summits providing hikers with breathtaking panoramic views. One of the most famous is Max Patch, offering 360-degree vistas that attract day-hikers and thru-hikers alike . Along the trail, hikers can explore the scenic Laurel Falls, enjoy the solitude at Beauty Spot and marvel at the historic graffiti left by Civil War soldiers in some of the caves along the route.

CHEROKEE NATIONAL FOREST
The Cherokee National Forest, named in honor of the Cherokee people who historically inhabited the region, stretches over 650,000 acres (263 hectares) in eastern Tennessee. This is about 2/3 the size of the state of Rhode Island, which is about 988,832 acres (400,166 hectares). The Cherokee utilized these lands for hunting, gathering and council meetings, making it a central part of their cultural and daily life.

European settlers began encroaching on these lands in the 18th century, bringing diseases and conflicts that devastated the Cherokee population. The most significant disruption came in 1838 when the Cherokee people were removed from their land. They were forcibly relocated to present-day Oklahoma. This tragic excursion, known as the Trail of Tears, resulted in the death of thousands of Cherokee during the journey and marked a profound loss of their ancestral homeland.

In the early 20th century, the U.S. government began purchasing land in the area to protect and restore it, following years of extensive logging and mining that had left the area heavily damaged and barren. The establishment of the Cherokee National Forest in 1920, along with the efforts of the Civilian Conservation Corps (CCC) in the 1930s, played a crucial role in revitalizing the forest. The CCC planted trees, built trails and constructed facilities, transforming the area into the beautiful and accessible forest that visitors enjoy today.

Today, Cherokee National Forest is a haven for outdoor lovers, offering more than 700 miles (1,126.5 km) of trails, including 150 miles (241 km) of the Appalachian National Scenic Trail. The forest is also home to diverse wildlife, including black bears, white-tailed deer and bald eagles.

EFFORTS TO RESTORE CHEROKEE LAND IN TENNESSEE

In recent years, efforts have been made to return some lands in Tennessee to the Cherokee. For instance, a congressional bill aims to transfer 76 acres along the Little Tennessee River back to the Eastern Band of Cherokee Indians. This land, historically significant to the Cherokee, is part of ongoing attempts to address past injustices and restore ancestral lands to Indigenous communities in Tennessee.

THE CASH CANYON OF TENNESSEE

The Tennessee River Gorge, known by the locals as "Cash Canyon" is a breathtaking natural treasure that covers 27,000 acres (10,926.5 hectares) and stretches 26 miles (41.8 km) through the Cumberland Mountains. To compare, Walt Disney World in Florida is 25,000 acres (10,117 hectares). This gorge is the fourth largest river canyon east of the Mississippi River and is known for its stunning scenery, rich biodiversity and fascinating history.

Tennessee River Gorge. Photo by Charlene N Simmons via Flickr

The gorge is home to thousands of plant species and a variety of wildlife, including bald eagles and river otters. Archaeological evidence suggests that humans have inhabited the gorge for at least 10,000 years, with ancient charcoal drawings found on cave walls.

The Tennessee River Blueway, a designated National Scenic River Trail, runs through the gorge and offers 46 miles (74 km) of navigable water for kayaking and canoeing.

5

TENNESSEE'S WILDLIFE & ANIMAL FACTS

OFFICIAL STATE BIRD: NORTHERN MOCKINGBIRD

Northern Mockingbird. Photo by steve_byland via depositphotos.com

The northern mockingbird was designated as Tennessee's official state bird in 1933, admired for its diverse songs and spirited presence.

Renowned for their impressive repertoire, northern mockingbirds can mimic the songs of other birds, as well as various sounds from their environment. These medium-sized gray birds with white patches on their wings are commonly found in open areas, from urban parks to rural fields. Known for their territorial behavior, they often sing throughout the day and even into the night.

OFFICIAL STATE WILD ANIMAL: RACCOON

The raccoon was designated as Tennessee's official state wild animal in 1971, celebrating its adaptability and prevalence across the state.

Recognizable by their distinctive black "mask" and ringed tail, raccoons are highly intelligent and resourceful mammals. They are omnivorous, with a diet that includes fruits, nuts, insects, and small animals. Raccoons are known for their dexterous front paws, which they use to manipulate objects and open containers. They also seem to wash their food before eating it. Raccoons have the ability to make over 50 different sounds that communicate different things.

They thrive in diverse habitats—from forests to urban areas—and are known for their curious and sometimes mischievous behavior.

DID YOU KNOW?
Tennessee's NFL team, the Tennessee Titans, have a raccoon as their mascot, called T-Rac.

OFFICIAL STATE INSECT: FIREFLY

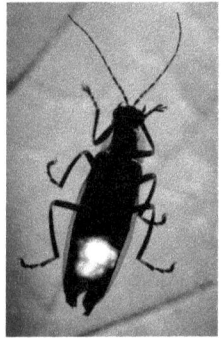

Firefly flashing. Photo by Fireflyphoto via depositphotos.com

The firefly, also known as the lightning bug, was designated as Tennessee's official state insect in 1975.

Celebrated for its enchanting bioluminescent display, these insects are a common sight during warm summer evenings. They illuminate the night with their flashing lights, which they use to attract mates. Fireflies thrive near bodies of water and in moist environments such as meadows and forests. Their larvae, known as glowworms, are beneficial predators of garden pests.

The magical light shows of fireflies are a beloved part of Tennessee's natural landscape, inspiring both wonder and scientific curiosity.

OFFICIAL STATE AGRICULTURAL INSECT: HONEYBEE

The honeybee was designated as Tennessee's official state agricultural insect in 1990, recognizing its crucial role in pollination and agriculture.

Honeybees are vital for pollinating a wide variety of crops. Known for their complex social structures, honeybees live in colonies with a single queen, numerous workers, and drones. They produce honey, which is harvested for food, and also beeswax, which is used in various products. Honeybees communicate through intricate dances to convey information about food sources.

OFFICIAL STATE BUTTERFLY: ZEBRA SWALLOWTAIL

Zebra Swallowtail butterfly. Photo by GeraldDeBoer via Depositphotos.com

The zebra swallowtail was designated as Tennessee's official state butterfly in 1995, and is admired for its striking appearance and grace.

Recognizable by its distinctive black and white striped wings, with extensions at the back that resemble tails, the zebra swallowtail is commonly found in wooded areas and near water sources where pawpaw trees grow. Pawpaw tress are the only species that host the larvae of zebra swallowtails. The adults feed on nectar from various flowers, showcasing their beauty as they flutter through gardens and forests.

OFFICIAL STATE REPTILE: EASTERN BOX TURTLE

The eastern box turtle was designated as Tennessee's official state reptile in 1995, highlighting its significance in the state's natural heritage.

Known for their highly domed, colorful shells with unique patterns, these turtles can live 30 to 40 years in the wild, with some reaching over 100 years in captivity. They have a hinged bottom portion of their shell, called the plastron, that allows them to close their shells completely for protection. Eastern box turtles are omnivorous, enjoying a diet of insects, worms, berries and plants.

They thrive in moist forests and meadows. During winter they brumate, a behavior similar to hibernating, by burrowing into soft soil. Conservation efforts focus on healthy habitats, because these turtles' declining populations are due to habitat destruction and road mortality.

OFFICIAL STATE SPORT FISH: SMALLMOUTH BASS

The smallmouth bass became Tennessee's official state sport fish in 2005 due to its popularity among anglers and its importance to the state's fishing culture.

Typically bronze to green in color with dark vertical bands along its side, smallmouth bass have a smaller mouth than large-mouth bass, with the upper jaw extending only to the middle of the eye. Known by nicknames like "bronzeback" and "smallie," they are prized for their strength, acrobatic jumps, and powerful runs.

The world-record smallmouth bass, weighing 11 lbs, 15 oz (5.4 kg), was caught by David Hayes in 1955 at Dale Hollow Lake, which straddles the Tennessee-Kentucky border. Smallmouth bass in the wild can live up to 15 years.

OFFICIAL STATE COMMERCIAL FISH: CHANNEL CATFISH

The channel catfish was designated as Tennessee's official state commercial fish in 1987, reflecting its importance to the state's fishing industry and culinary traditions.

Known for their distinctive whisker-like barbels around the mouth, channel catfish are commonly found in freshwater rivers, lakes, and streams throughout Tennessee. They are a popular target for anglers due to their size, abundance, and fighting spirit. Channel catfish have a varied diet, feeding on insects, crustaceans, and plant material. They are also a staple in Southern cuisine, often featured in dishes such as fried catfish.

OFFICIAL STATE HORSE: TENNESSEE WALKING HORSE

The Tennessee Walking Horse is a calm and gentle breed that was developed in the Central Basin of Tennessee during the late 18th century and is known for its smooth, four-beat "running walk." This gait provides a very comfortable ride, making it ideal for long distances.

The breed was developed by crossing Narragansett Pacers, Canadian Pacers, Thoroughbreds, Morgans, and Standardbreds.

The breed is celebrated annually at the National Tennessee Walking Horse Celebration in Shelbyville, which is one of the state's largest and most popular events.

Midnight Sun, a two-time World Grand Champion (1945 and 1946), is one of the most famous Tennessee Walking Horses. His influence on the breed is substantial, and many modern Walking Horses can trace their lineage back to him.

THE SALAMANDER CAPITAL

The Great Smoky Mountains National Park in Tennessee has been called the "Salamander Capital of the World." It is home to 30 different species of salamanders, more than any other single location on Earth.

Many of the salamanders found in Tennessee, such as the Red-cheeked salamander, are lungless. They breathe entirely through their skin and the lining of their mouth, which requires them to live in damp environments to keep their skin moist.

Salamanders in Tennessee range from the tiny Pygmy salamander, which is just over an inch long, to the impressively large Hellbender, which can grow up to 29 inches. The Hellbender is the largest aquatic salamander in North America and can be found in the clean, fast-flowing waters of Tennessee.

The Hellbender has several less-than-appealing nicknames, including "snot otter," "lasagna lizard," and "old slippery," referring to its distinct appearance and slippery skin.

SYNCHRONOUS FIREFLIES

Synchronous Fireflies. Photo by Danae Wolfe/Chasing Bugs (chasingbugs.com)

The Great Smoky Mountains National Park is one of the few places in the world where you can see the mesmerizing display of synchronous fireflies.

These fireflies are one of the few species in the world that can synchronize their flashing light patterns. The males fly and flash and the females respond with a flash. The synchronous flashing is thought to be a mating ritual, where males attract females with patterned flashing; this makes it easier for females to locate males of their own species in the dense forest.

This event occurs annually for about two weeks in late May to early June. Because this natural phenomenon is so popular, the National Park Service has a lottery system for viewing. Visitors must apply for a pass during the application period in April to visit the viewing area during the peak season in late spring.

BAT COLONIES

Tennessee is home to at least 16 different bat species, some of which live in colonies numbering in the hundreds of thousands. Bats play a vital role in the ecosystem by controlling insect populations. This means they also contribute significantly to Tennessee's agriculture. Their insatiable appetite for insects is estimated to save U.S. farmers billions of dollars annually by reducing the need for pesticides.

One of the most famous bat colonies in Tennessee resides in Nickajack Cave near Chattanooga. Every evening during the warmer months, visitors can witness thousands of bats exiting the cave at dusk, a spectacular natural event. This colony primarily consists of Gray bats, an endangered species.

BEAR COUNTRY

Black bear in Cades Cove, Tennessee. Photo by Tom Shockey via Flickr

Tennessee is home to an estimated 1,500 black bears, one of the largest populations in the Eastern U.S.

Primarily located in the Great Smoky Mountains, black bears can also be found in other parts of East Tennessee, including the Cherokee National Forest and the Big South Fork National River and Recreation Area.

BEAR BASICS

Bears are typically solitary animals, although they may gather in groups to feed on a particularly abundant food source.

Bears are generally considered intelligent animals, and they have been known to use tools, solve problems and even show empathy toward other bears.

Male bears are called boars, females are called sows and young bears are cubs.

BLACK BEARS
Black bears are the smallest of the North American bears. Adults are about 29 inches (73 cm) at the shoulders when on all fours and measure about 60 inches (152 cm) from nose to tail. Adult males normally weigh about 180–200 pounds (81–90 kg).

Black bears aren't always black. They can be jet black, bluish black, brown, cinnamon-colored, and even white, though black is the most common. In Tennessee, these color variations are less common but can be seen in Tennessee's black bear population.

ONLY BLACK BEARS IN TENNESSEE
You won't find grizzly bears in Tennessee. Grizzly bears are native to the western United States, particularly in states like Montana, Wyoming, and Alaska, and do not inhabit the eastern forests of Tennessee.

BEARS NOT ONLY FLOAT, BUT CAN SWIM
Having high fat content and an oily fur coat makes it easy for hefty bears to stay afloat and swim. Black bears are excellent swimmers and are often seen swimming in the rivers and lakes of Tennessee. They swim to cool off, find food, or escape danger.

SKILLFUL CLIMBERS
Black bears are agile climbers. They can climb trees quickly and often do so to escape predators, find food or rest. Young bears, in particular, spend a lot of time in trees.

TRAVELING BEARS
Black bears can travel long distances in search of food, mates or new territory. Some bears have been known to wander over 100 miles (160.9 km) from their original home range.

BEAR MIGRATION
Some black bears in Tennessee exhibit seasonal migration patterns, moving to lower elevations during the winter and returning to higher elevations in the spring and summer. This movement is often driven by food availability and weather conditions.

THE BLACK BEAR DIET
In addition to berries and nuts, black bears in Tennessee enjoy a diverse diet that includes acorns, honey, carrion and even insects like ants and bees. They are also known to eat amphibians and reptiles when available.

BEAR ENCOUNTERS
Despite their size, black bears are generally shy and avoid human contact. Most encounters with bears in Tennessee result in the bear fleeing the area. Bear attacks are extremely rare and typically occur only when the bear feels threatened or cornered.

GIANT FRESHWATER DRUM FISH
Tennessee's waters are home to the freshwater drum, the only member of the drum family that inhabits fresh water. These fish can grow to over 30 inches long and weigh more than 35 pounds (15.8 kg).

The giant freshwater drum is also commonly referred to as the sheepshead, croaker or grunter.

Freshwater drum are named for the drumming sound they produce by vibrating their swim bladder. This sound is often used during the spawning season to attract mates. These fish can live a long time, often reaching 13 years or more in the wild. Some individuals have been known to live over 70 years.

AMERICAN BALD EAGLES

Once endangered, the American bald eagle has made a significant comeback in Tennessee. These majestic birds can often be seen soaring over lakes and rivers, especially during the winter months when they migrate to the area. In Tennessee, they are often found around large bodies of water like Reelfoot Lake, where they nest in tall trees. Bald eagles build some of the largest bird nests, known as eyries, which can be up to 13 feet (3.9 meters) deep and 8 feet (2.4 meters) wide.

DID YOU KNOW?
Each January, Reelfoot Lake hosts the Eagle Festival, where visitors can observe bald eagles in their natural habitat. The festival includes guided eagle tours, photography workshops and educational programs about birds of prey.

ELK
Elk were reintroduced to Tennessee in 2001 in the Cumberland Plateau, an effort that involved transporting 201 elk from Canada.

Elk had been absent from Tennessee for nearly 150 years. The best places to see elk in Tennessee are the Hatfield Knob Viewing Area and the North Cumberland Wildlife Management Area.

RED FOX

The red fox is common throughout Tennessee and is known for its cunning behavior and adaptability to both wild and urban environments. They are easily recognizable by their reddish fur and bushy tails. They live in family groups consisting of a pair and their offspring.

COYOTES

Coyotes are highly adaptable and are found throughout Tennessee. Coyotes are known for their vocalizations, which include howls, yips and barks to communicate with each other at night. They can thrive in diverse environments, from rural farmland to inner-city neighborhoods.

RIVER OTTERS

River otters are playful and social animals that have made a comeback in Tennessee waterways. They are excellent swimmers and are often seen sliding down riverbanks or playing in the water. They are capable of holding their breath for several minutes while hunting for fish and crustaceans.

BARN OWLS

Barn owls are known for their heart-shaped faces and eerie, raspy screeches. They are excellent hunters and help control rodent populations in rural areas. Their feathers are adapted for silent flight, allowing them to sneak up on prey undetected. They often nest in barns, abandoned buildings, and tree cavities, making them common in both rural and suburban areas.

6

TENNESSEE'S TREES AND PLANTS

OFFICIAL STATE TREE: TULIP POPLAR

Closeup of the Tulip Poplar tree flower. Image by yana.demenko via depositphotos.com

Belonging to the magnolia family, rather than the poplar family, the Tulip has been Tennessee's official state tree since 1947. The tree stands out for its towering height, reaching over 150 feet (45.7 meters), and its distinctive tulip-like flowers. It was chosen as the official state tree "because it grows from one end of the state to the other."

Native Americans used the tree's bark to make medicine and constructed canoes from its trunks. The Tulip Poplar was highly valued by early European settlers for building homes and furniture due to its tall, straight growth and workable wood.

OFFICIAL STATE EVERGREEN TREE: EASTERN RED CEDAR

In 2012, Tennessee named the Eastern Red Cedar as the state evergreen tree. It's not actually a cedar tree, but a juniper tree. They normally grow as big, bushy shrubs and their trunks aren't usually exposed unless trimmed and trained. It's admired for its hardy nature and aromatic wood and is found throughout the entire state.

Historically, its wood was used by early settlers for fence posts and cedar chests due to its resistance to decay and insects. The tree, a symbol of resilience, is sacred to the Cherokee people, and its wood is often used in traditional ceremonies and crafts.

DOGWOOD TREES

The flowering dogwood is a popular ornamental tree in Tennessee, known for its delicate white or pink blossoms. It is the state tree of neighboring North Carolina.

THE AMERICAN CHESTNUT TREE

Once a dominant species in Tennessee's Appalachian forests, the American Chestnut grew over 100 feet (30 meters) tall and was vital to the region's ecosystem and economy. A fungal blight in the early 1900s killed over four billion trees across the U.S., nearly wiping out the species by the 1940s, including in the Great Smoky Mountains. Today, organizations like The American Chestnut Foundation are working to breed blight-resistant trees, with hopes of restoring them to Tennessee's forests.

THE INVASIVE KUDZU VINE

Kudzu in Tennessee. Photo by Laurie Hulsey via Flickr.

Tennessee is no stranger to the invasive Kudzu vine. Known as "the vine that ate the South," Kudzu can rapidly overtake and cover entire landscapes, including trees, buildings, and roadsides. The vine is considered one of the most invasive plant species in the United States.

Kudzu was introduced to the United States from Japan during the late 19th century as an ornamental plant and erosion-control method. It was promoted as a forage crop and used in Civilian Conservation Corps (CCC) projects.

While Kudzu is considered a nuisance, some people have discovered creative uses for it. The leaves and young shoots of Kudzu can be harvested and used in cooking, often in recipes inspired by Asian cuisines. Kudzu root has also been used in traditional medicine for its potential health benefits.

The Vine that Ate the South. Photo by Casey Fox via Flickr

DID YOU KNOW?
Kudzu Covered Buildings
In many instances, Kudzu has overtaken abandoned buildings

or structures in Tennessee. These peculiar scenes have prompted amusing comments and comparisons, with some people referring to the structures as "Kudzu condos" or "Kudzu castles."

OFFICIAL STATE FRUIT

Tomatoes, despite often being considered vegetables, are botanically fruits. This is because they develop from a flowering plant's ovary and contain seeds. In Tennessee, tomatoes are integral to the state's culinary traditions, featuring prominently in dishes like fried green tomatoes, tomato sandwiches and tomato-based sauces. The tomato was designated the official state fruit in 2003.

Several colorful festivals involving tomatoes are held in Tennessee, but the Tomato Art Fest in Nashville is a well-known and quirky celebration of all things tomato. The festival includes tomato-themed art, music, food vendors and a tomato parade, attracting visitors from near and far to join in the fun.

OFFICIAL STATE FLOWER: IRIS

The Iris, Tennessee's official state cultivated flower since 1933, is celebrated for its diverse colors and elegant appearance, symbolizing the state's natural beauty and cultural heritage. Chosen for its widespread presence across Tennessee and its role in garden and landscape design, the Iris reflects the state's rich flora. The Iris comes in many colors, but the purple Iris is considered the state flower.

PASSION FLOWER

The Passion Flower, is one of Tennessee's treasured wild blooms, also fondly known as Maypop, Wild Apricot and by its Cherokee name, Ocoee, which means apricot vine plant.

Tennessee Coneflower. Photo by Masebrock, Public domain, via Wikimedia Commons.

TENNESSEE CONEFLOWER

The Tennessee coneflower, once thought extinct, was rediscovered in the 1960s and listed as endangered in 1979. Native to the unique limestone glades of Middle Tennessee, its striking purple petals and orange core make it a standout wildflower. After decades of conservation efforts by The Nature Conservancy, the U.S. Fish and Wildlife Service, and other partners, the Tennessee coneflower recovered enough to be removed from the endangered species list in 2011.

TENNESSEE'S TREES AND PLANTS

RHODODENDRONS IN THE SMOKIES
The Great Smoky Mountains National Park is home to a stunning display of Rhododendron blooms. The park boasts the largest natural stand of native Great Rhododendron in the world, creating breathtaking scenes of vibrant pink and purple flowers.

WILD ONION
The wild onion, found in the woodlands of Tennessee, is a pungent and flavorful plant that's been used both culinarily and medicinally by native peoples for centuries. These onions bloom with a distinctive white or purple flower and can be used much like their cultivated cousins.

American Persimmons. Photo by Jianghongyan via depositphotos.com.

AMERICAN PERSIMMON
Persimmons in Tennessee ripen to a sweet, honey-like flavor after the first frost. Native American tribes crafted a bread from the fruit, a tradition still honored in some Southern kitchens.

Interestingly, persimmon seeds are used by some to predict winter weather, with the shape inside forecasting snow—a knife shape indicates cutting cold, whereas a spoon shape says shoveling snow is on the way.

PAWPAW

The Pawpaw, America's forgotten fruit, is indigenous to Tennessee and has a tropical flavor reminiscent of bananas and mangoes. Pawpaws have more protein than most other fruits and were a staple in Native American diets. Each fall, Tennesseans celebrate this custard-like fruit at local festivals.

EASTERN PRICKLY PEAR

The Eastern Prickly Pear is a hardy cactus native to the eastern U.S., including Tennessee, and is notable for its low-growing, clump-forming shape with round, purplish-green pads. In late spring, it blooms with bright yellow to gold flowers, sometimes with a red center. This cactus is resilient and can thrive in most of Tennessee's counties.

BLACK HUCKLEBERRY

Huckleberries in Tennessee are a late-summer delight, much smaller than their cousin, the blueberry, but with a similar taste. These little berries, often found on the higher ridges, add a burst of sweetness to the palate of hikers and wildlife alike. Picking huckleberries is often a cherished seasonal activity, with family traditions built around harvesting these wild treats.

GOOSEBERRIES

Gooseberries. Photo by NataliiaMeInyc via depositphotos.com

Gooseberries are less common but can be identified by their greenish color and tart flavor. Tennessee's Gooseberries are a blend of tart culinary and sweet dessert varieties, versatile for both savory and sweet dishes. These hardy plants thrive locally, bearing fruit for decades. This is a testament to their low-maintenance nature. They tend to grow alongside other wild berries and make for a tart snack or a wonderful addition to jams and pies.

BLACKBERRY

Tennessee's wild blackberries are a summer delight, ripening in June. These juicy gems are packed with antioxidants and are often found dotting the scenic byways and open fields across the state.

TENNESSEE GREENS AND HERBS

Tennessee's wild greens, including dandelion, mustard and poke have long been foraged for traditional "messes of greens." These greens are often cooked down with a piece of pork for a Southern delicacy. Herbs like wild mint and mountain mint spice up the local flora and are used to brew soothing teas.

CHRISTMAS TREE FARMS

Tennessee has around 30 Christmas Tree farms throughout the state. These farms let you find and cut your own tree, choose one that's already been cut or select one that's been balled and burlapped at the roots, making it easy to keep the tree alive and transplant after the holidays.

Christmas trees grown in Tennessee include: Eastern White Pine, Fraser Fir, Leyland Cypress, Norway Spruce, Scotch Pine, Virginia Pine, Arizona Cypress Blue Ice, Arizona Cypress Carolina Sapphire, Canaan Fir, Colorado Blue Spruce, and the Concolor Fir.

7
TENNESSEE'S PEOPLE & POPULATION

TENNESSEE'S POPULATION
As of 2023, the population of Tennessee was estimated to be 7,126,400, reflecting a growth from the 2022 estimate of 7,048,900. Tennessee ranks as the 16th most populous U.S. state.

WHERE MOST TENNESSEAN'S LIVE
With roughly 678,000 people, the capitol city of Nashville is the most populated city in Tennessee. The Nashville metro area, which includes 14 counties, has about 2.04 million people as of 2022.

Memphis ranks number two, with roughly 630,000 people. Third place goes to Knoxville with around 200,300 people.

THE LEAST POPULATED TENNESSEE TOWN
Nestled east of Memphis near the Tennessee-Mississippi border, Saulsbury stands out for its small population. Located

in Hardeman County, the town holds the title of the least populated town in Tennessee, with just 81 residents.

TENNESSEE MILLIONAIRES
In Tennessee, there are more than 130,000 millionaire households, indicating combined homes and assets worth at least $1 million. This concentration of millionaires is about 5% of the state's total population, which is below the national U.S. average.

TENNESSEE BILLIONAIRES
As of 2023, Tennessee is home to 11 billionaires, with wealth stemming from various industries such as healthcare, finance and retail.

SOUTHERN HOSPITALITY
Tennesseans are known for their warm and welcoming nature, often exemplifying the legendary Southern hospitality. Visitors often remark on the friendly demeanor of the state's residents.

SPIRIT OF VOLUNTEERISM
Tennessee embraces a strong spirit of volunteerism. According to data from the Corporation for National and Community Service, the state consistently ranks among the top states in terms of volunteer rates and hours served.

DISTINCT ACCENTS
Various regional accents can be heard throughout Tennessee, reflecting the state's diverse cultural influences. From the Appalachian-heavy speech in the eastern part of the state to the distinct drawl in areas like Memphis, these accents add to the diverse linguistic tapestry of Tennessee.

Appalachian Influence: The eastern part of Tennessee, nestled within the Appalachian Mountains, showcases accents produced by the region's Scotch-Irish settlers. These accents are characterized by a distinctive twang and vocabulary, reflecting the area's rich cultural heritage. Hear a sample at: https://tinyurl.com/appalachian-english-video

Memphis Drawl: In cities like Memphis, a deep Southern drawl can be heard, influenced by the city's history as a major hub for the cotton and blues industries. This drawl is often characterized by elongated vowels and a relaxed pace of speech, reflecting the laid-back vibe of the region. Hear a sample here: https://tinyurl.com/memphis-accent

Nashville's Melting Pot: Nashville, as the capital and cultural center of Tennessee, boasts a diverse population, leading to a blend of accents from various regions. You might hear a mix of Southern drawls, Midwest twangs, and even hints of Northern accents, reflecting the city's status as a melting pot of cultures and influences. Hear a sample at: https://tinyurl.com/Nashville-accent

Influence of African American Vernacular English (AAVE): Throughout Tennessee, especially in urban areas, you'll find influences from African American Vernacular English (AAVE) in the local accents. This reflects the significant contributions of African American communities to the cultural fabric of the state, particularly in music, food and language.

Here some examples at: https://tinyurl.com/aave-examples

MELUNGEONS

The Melungeons are a tri-racial group with European, African, and Native American ancestry, primarily found in Hancock and Hawkins counties, Tennessee.

The term "Melungeon" likely comes from the French word "mélange," meaning mixture, reflecting their mixed heritage.

They often have olive or darker skin, high cheekbones, straight black hair, and light-colored eyes.

The Melungeons blend European, African and Native American traditions in their music, storytelling and food.

Newman's Ridge in Hancock County is a notable Melungeon settlement, providing a place for the community to live relatively undisturbed.

The people here have a distinct blend of dialects and rich oral traditions that have preserved their history.

Some notable individuals believed to have Melungeon ancestry include Elvis Presley, Abraham Lincoln, and Ava Gardner. While these claims are often debated, they highlight the widespread interest in Melungeon heritage.

The Melungeon Heritage Association was founded to preserve and promote the history and culture of the Melungeon people. They hold annual gatherings known as "Unions" to celebrate their heritage and share research.

TENNESSEE'S ORIGINAL INHABITANTS
The original inhabitants of Tennessee included several Native American tribes, primarily the Cherokee, Chickasaw, Shawnee and Creek.

CHEROKEE NATION
The Cherokee were one of the largest and most significant tribes in Tennessee. Known for their advanced political and social systems, the Cherokee lived in large, organized towns throughout the southeastern United States, including the states of Tennessee, North Carolina and Georgia.

The Cherokee were skilled farmers, hunters and craftsmen, and developed a written language and a constitution modeled after the United States. The Cherokee towns in Tennessee included Chota and Tanasi, which played vital roles in their cultural and political life.

THE CHICKASAW
The Chickasaw were another prominent tribe in Tennessee, inhabiting the western part of the state. They were known as fierce warriors and practiced hunters, farmers and traders. The Chickasaw lived in fortified villages along rivers and were experienced at navigating the waterways of the region.

THE SHAWNEE
While the Shawnee were not as prominently settled in Tennessee as the other tribes, they had significant interactions with the region, especially in the central and northern parts. The Shawnee were excellent hunters and warriors, and had a rich oral tradition and cultural heritage.

THE CREEK

The Creek, also known as the Muscogee, occupied parts of southeastern Tennessee and areas in Alabama and Georgia. They were a confederacy of several smaller tribes, each with its own distinct culture but united under a central leadership. The Creek were known for their complex societies, with established towns and economies based on agriculture, hunting and trade.

TRAIL OF TEARS

The Cherokee were among the last Native American groups to inhabit the region before the Indian Removal Act of 1830 forced them and other tribes to relocate to what is now Oklahoma.

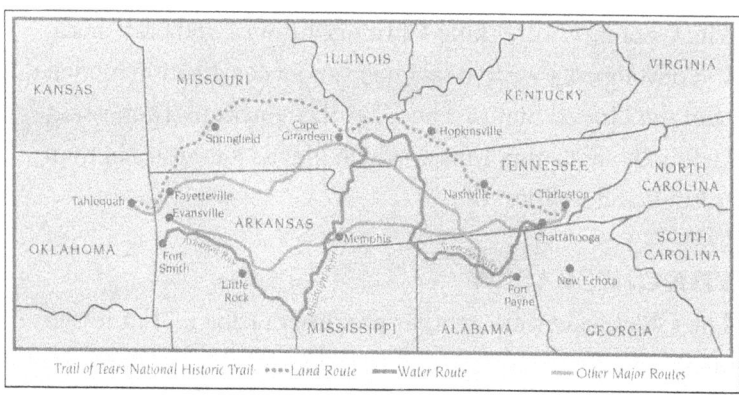

Map of the Trail of Tears. Image by the National Park Service. Public Domain. Wikimedia.org.

This tragic journey—now known as the Trail of Tears—took place from 1838 to 1839, and profoundly impacted Tennessee. Approximately 16,000 Cherokee were forcibly removed from their homes, and about 4,000 died due to harsh conditions along the journey to Oklahoma, including disease, starvation and exhaustion. The Trail of Tears is remembered for its severe human suffering and the resilience of the Cherokee people.

MULTIPLE TRIBES AFFECTED

While the Cherokee are the tribe most associated with the Trail of Tears, they were not the only ones affected. The Choctaw, Creek (Muscogee), Seminole and Chickasaw tribes were also forcibly removed from their homelands.

HISTORICAL RECOGNITION

The Trail of Tears is a system of routes covering approximately 2,200 miles (3,540 km) across nine states, and was designated a National Historic Trail in 1987. This designation helps preserve the memory and educate the public about this dark chapter in American history, ensuring that the suffering and resilience of the Native American tribes are not forgotten.

Despite this forced removal, the legacy of these tribes remains an integral part of Tennessee's history and culture.

EASTERN BAND OF CHEROKEE

Not all Cherokee were removed. Several hundred evaded capture by hiding in the Great Smoky Mountains, eventually forming the Eastern Band of Cherokee Indians, who still reside in North Carolina today.

8

TENNESSEE CULTURE & SOUTHERN HOSPITALITY

Southern hospitality in Tennessee is all about making people feel welcome, cherished and part of the community. From warm welcomes to delicious food, from polite manners to vibrant festivals, it's a culture rich with tradition and kindness. Whether you're a resident or a visitor, you'll find that the spirit of Southern hospitality is alive and well in the Volunteer State.

WARM WELCOMES AND GENEROSITY

In Tennessee, you'll find that people take hospitality seriously. A visit to a Southern home almost always starts with a warm smile and a hearty greeting. Guests are quickly offered sweet tea and invited to relax. It's not just about being polite; it's about making sure everyone feels like they belong. So, whether you're a longtime friend or a first-time visitor, expect to be treated like family.

COOKING AND FOOD TRADITIONS

Food is at the heart of Southern hospitality, and Tennessee's culinary traditions are no exception. Meals are often made from scratch, with recipes passed down through generations. Think fried chicken, collard greens, cornbread and pecan pie. These dishes aren't just food; they're a way of bringing people together. Family gatherings, community potlucks and Sunday dinners are filled with laughter, storytelling, and—of course—delicious food.

FRONT PORCH SITTING

One of the most iconic images of Southern life is the front porch. In Tennessee, the front porch is more than just an architectural feature; it's a social hub. Evenings are often spent sitting on the porch, sipping sweet tea and chatting with neighbors. It's a place for reflection, relaxation and building community. So, don't be surprised if you're invited to "sit a spell" when you visit a Tennessee home.

FAMILY AND COMMUNITY

Family ties and community connections run deep in Tennessee. Family gatherings are frequent and lively, often extending to include friends and neighbors. Sundays are particularly special, with large family dinners that bring everyone together. It's common for entire communities to come together for events, whether it's a church picnic, a local fair or a charity fundraiser. This sense of belonging and support is a cornerstone of Southern hospitality.

POTLUCK DINNERS

In Tennessee, the potluck dinner is a beloved tradition. Friends, family and community members gather together. They each bring a dish to share, creating a diverse and delicious feast.

These gatherings are common at church functions, family reunions and community events. It's a wonderful way to showcase culinary talents and enjoy a variety of homemade dishes. Plus, it perfectly embodies the Southern values of sharing and community.

QUILTING BEES

Quilting bees. Photo by Bisse Bowman via Flickr

Quilting bees are a longstanding tradition where friends and family gather to work on quilts together. These social gatherings are as much about community bonding as they are about creating beautiful, hand-made quilts. Whether for weddings, new babies or fundraising events, quilting bees showcase the skill, creativity and collaborative spirit that are hallmarks of Southern life.

FAITH AND CHURCH
Faith plays a significant role in the lives of many Tennesseans. Church is more than a place of worship. It's also a center of community life. Sunday services, Bible studies and church picnics are common occurrences. Churches often organize events that bring people together, fostering a sense of unity and shared purpose. The church is where many find not only spiritual guidance but also lifelong friendships.

POLITENESS AND ETIQUETTE
Manners are a big deal in Tennessee. From a young age, children are taught to say "please," "thank you," "yes, ma'am," and "no, sir." This emphasis on politeness extends to all interactions, making everyday encounters pleasant and respectful. Whether you're at a grocery store or a formal event, you can expect to be treated with courtesy and kindness. It's all part of that famous Southern charm.

CELEBRATIONS AND FESTIVALS
Tennessee loves a good celebration. Festivals, fairs and parades are regular events that highlight local culture, food, music and traditions. From the world-famous Bonnaroo Music and Arts Festival to small-town county fairs, there's always something to celebrate. These events are vibrant, lively and a great way to experience the best of Southern hospitality.

DECORATION DAY
An enduring Southern tradition, Decoration Day predates Memorial Day and is widely observed in Tennessee.

Originating in the 19th century, families gather at cemeteries to honor deceased loved ones by cleaning and decorating their graves with fresh flowers and wreaths. This event is also a social occasion, often including picnics, storytelling and religious services. Unlike Memorial Day—which honors military personnel—Decoration Day is more inclusive, celebrating all deceased family members. This tradition is still observed across the Southern U.S., not just in Tennessee.

At cemeteries across Tennessee, such as the historic Old Gray Cemetery in Knoxville, Decoration Day remains a significant event. Often, Decoration Day is celebrated the Sunday before Memorial Day in May and may be called Decoration Sunday.

STORYTELLING AND FOLKLORE
Storytelling is a cherished tradition in Tennessee. Gatherings often involve sharing tales of family history, local legends and personal anecdotes. These stories are more than just entertainment; they're a way of preserving history and connecting generations. Whether it's around a campfire or at a family reunion, storytelling brings people together and keeps the past alive.

SHIVAREE (CHIVAREE)
Shivaree, sometimes called chivaree, is a playful Southern tradition involving newlyweds. Friends and neighbors gather outside the newly married couple's home on the wedding night to create a loud, joyous commotion with pots, pans and musical instruments. The ruckus was believed to bring good luck and blessings to the new marriage. Though less common now, it remains a charming part of Tennessee's cultural history.

BLESS YOUR HEART
The phrase "bless your heart" is a quintessential part of Southern speech, especially in Tennessee. It's a versatile expression that can convey genuine sympathy or a gentle reprimand. If someone says, "Well, bless your heart," it could mean

they feel for your situation or that they're acknowledging a blunder with kindness. It's all about the context and tone.

FIXIN' TO

In Tennessee, people are often "fixin' to" do something. This phrase means getting ready to take action. If you hear, "I'm fixin' to head out," it means the person is about to leave. It's a charming way to express intention and is a common part of everyday conversation.

MIGHT COULD

"Might could" is another delightful Southern expression you'll hear in Tennessee. It indicates a possibility, combining "might" and "could" for extra emphasis. For example, "I might could help you with that later" suggests that the speaker is considering helping, but it's not a definite commitment. It's a way of keeping options open and conversations polite.

9

INDUSTRY AND ECONOMY

MUSIC INDUSTRY
Known as "Music City," Nashville is a global center for the music industry, particularly country music. In fact, Nashville isn't just the country music capital; it's a whole vibe. You've got the Grand Ole Opry, the Country Music Hall of Fame, the Country Hall of Fame, historic Ryman Auditorium, numerous recording studios and a live music scene that's popping every night. Strolling down Broadway, you'll find honky-tonks playing tunes from morning till night.

Tennessee's music industry contributes over $5 billion to the state's economy, supporting over 60,000 jobs and drawing millions of tourists each year.

HANDMADE GUITARS
Tennessee is home to several renowned guitar manufacturers, including Gibson Guitars, which has been crafting high-quality instruments in Nashville since 1902. These guitars are highly sought after by musicians worldwide.

INDUSTRY AND ECONOMY

AUTOMOTIVE HUB
Tennessee is a significant player in the automotive industry, hosting major manufacturing plants for both Nissan (in Smyrna) and Volkswagen (in Chattanooga). Nissan's Smyrna automotive plant is one of the largest in North America, producing over 600,000 vehicles annually.

LOGISTICS AND TRANSPORTATION
Tennessee's central location makes it a critical logistics and transportation hub. Memphis is known as "America's Distribution Center" due to its strategic location and extensive logistics infrastructure. It features the world's second-busiest cargo airport, because it is home to FedEx's global headquarters.

FISH FARMING
Tennessee is a leading producer of farm-raised catfish, particularly in the western part of the state. Aquaculture contributes significantly to the local economies of rural communities.

AGRICULTURE
Agriculture remains a vital part of Tennessee's economy. The state is a top producer of soybeans, cotton and corn. Tennessee is also known for its tobacco, which has been a staple crop since colonial times. Livestock farming, particularly beef cattle, is another key component of the agricultural sector, with Tennessee ranking high in beef production.

Agriculture contributes around $3.5 billion annually to Tennessee's economy and supports over 67,000 farms.

HEALTHCARE HUBS

Nashville is home to more than 500 healthcare companies, making it a leading city for healthcare management. HCA Healthcare, headquartered in Nashville, is one of the largest hospital operators in the world.

The healthcare sector in Tennessee employs over 400,000 people, making it one of the largest job creators in the state.

WHISKEY PRODUCTION

Lynchburg, Tennessee, is home to the Jack Daniel's Distillery, the oldest registered distillery in the United States. Jack Daniel's Tennessee Whiskey is known worldwide and is a major tourist attraction. The Tennessee Whiskey Trail includes over 30 distilleries, showcasing the state's rich tradition of whiskey production, which contributes to tourism and the local economies.

DID YOU KNOW?
Whiskey or Whisky? What's the difference?

The spelling difference between "whiskey" and "whisky" began in the 1870s, when Irish distillers added an "e" to distinguish their product from Scottish versions. The U.S. followed Ireland's lead, while Scotland, Canada, and Japan kept the original "whisky" spelling. Today, the "e" is mainly used in Ireland and the U.S., while other countries continue to use "whisky."

A helpful way to remember this is that countries with an "E" in their name, like Ireland and the United States, tend to use "whiskey," while countries without an "E," like Scotland and Canada, stick with "whisky."

TOURISM

Come for the music, stay for the mountains! Tennessee is a haven for music enthusiasts and nature lovers alike.

Tennessee is a treasure trove of natural beauty, cultural landmarks and historical sites, making it a top destination for tourists. Tennessee's tourism industry attracts over 100 million visitors each year, people who are drawn to the state's rich musical heritage and breathtaking natural landscapes. Visitors can explore the vibrant music scenes in Nashville and Memphis, hike through the Great Smoky Mountains National Park and discover the historical charm of small towns and Civil War sites.

The tourism industry supports businesses and jobs across Tennessee, contributing significantly to the state's economy. Here are the top three tourist sites in Tennessee:

The Great Smoky Mountains National Park is the most-visited national park in the United States, attracting over 12 million visitors annually. The park straddles the border between Tennessee and North Carolina and offers stunning scenery, diverse wildlife and over 800 miles (1,287 km) of hiking trails.

Dollywood, located in Pigeon Forge, is one of the top theme parks in the U.S., drawing about 3 million visitors each year. Owned by country music star Dolly

Parton, the park features rides, shows and festivals celebrating Appalachian culture.

Graceland, Elvis Presley's former home in Memphis is a must-visit for music fans. Over 600,000 fans from around the world visit each year. Graceland gives you a glimpse into the life of the King of Rock 'n' Roll and is packed with memorabilia, gold records and some seriously cool jumpsuits.

NASCAR RACING

NASCAR racing is a significant industry in Tennessee, contributing to the state's economy and cultural identity. With its iconic tracks, legendary drivers and passionate fanbase, NASCAR has a deep-rooted presence in the Volunteer State.

Major NASCAR events draw hundreds of thousands of visitors annually. These tourists contribute to the local economy through spending on hotels, restaurants, retail and entertainment. Bristol Motor Speedway's events alone bring in millions of dollars each year.

DID YOU KNOW?

NASCAR is an abbreviation for National Association for Stock Car Auto Racing.

AGRITOURISM

Agritourism is a growing industry in Tennessee, with farms offering activities like corn mazes, pumpkin patches and vineyard tours. This trend helps support local agriculture while providing exhilarating experiences for visitors.

TECHNOLOGY HUBS
Nashville and Chattanooga are emerging as technology hubs, home to a growing number of tech startups and innovation centers. Chattanooga, known as "Gig City," was the first city in the U.S. to offer gigabit internet speeds to its residents.

TENNESSEE RIVER PEARLS
The Tennessee River is known for producing some of the largest freshwater pearls in North America. The Tennessee River Freshwater Pearl Farm in Camden is the only freshwater pearl culturing farm in the country.

NO STATE INCOME TAXES
Tennessee is one of nine U.S. states that doesn't have income taxes. This means residents get to keep a lot more of their paychecks.

MINIMUM WAGE IN TENNESSEE
As of 2024, the minimum wage in Tennessee is $7.25, which is the same as the federal minimum wage.

10

TENNESSEE & SPORTS

NO OFFICIAL STATE SPORT
Tennessee might not have an official state sport, but that doesn't mean the Volunteer State isn't packed with action. American football's a big deal here, with fans flocking to see the Tennessee Volunteers and the NFL's Tennessee Titans (NFL stands for National Football League and refers to American Football). Basketball also gets a lot of love, especially with the Memphis Grizzlies and the legendary Lady Vols. And let's not forget the adrenaline-pumping NASCAR races at Bristol Motor Speedway.

For outdoor fun, Tennessee's has great spots for fishing, hunting, hiking and boating. So, whether you're into team sports or outdoor adventures, Tennessee's got you covered.

FOOTBALL FRENZY
Dive into the football frenzy of Tennessee, where both college and professional teams ignite the spirit of the Volunteer State.

TENNESSEE & SPORTS

In Tennessee, football is more than just a game, it's a way of life.

TENNESSEE TITANS

The Tennessee Titans, based in Nashville, have captivated football fans since their relocation from Houston, Texas in 1997. Originally called the Oilers, they had a rich history tied to the Texas oil industry, even featuring an oil derrick on their helmets.

However, financial challenges and stadium issues in Houston prompted team owner Bud Adams to seek a new home, ultimately choosing Tennessee. The team played its first two seasons in Memphis and at Vanderbilt Stadium in Nashville before being renamed the Titans in 1999 and moving to their permanent home at Nissan Stadium.

The sword is a symbol of the Titans' mascot, T-Rac, a cartoonish version of a raccoon. The state's official wild animal represents the team's fighting spirit. Titans games are known for their unique traditions, including the "Sword of Honor," a pregame ritual where a selected person gets to unsheathe the sword on the field, symbolizing readiness for battle.

COLLEGE FOOTBALL

In Tennessee, college football is a big deal. The University of Tennessee Volunteers, affectionately known as the Vols, are the team leading the charge.

The Vols have a rich and celebrated past filled with significant achievements, memorable events and notable traditions. Dating back to 1891, the Volunteers boast over 800 wins, making them one of the winningest programs in NCAA (National Collegiate Athletic Association) history.

On gamedays, Neyland Stadium in Knoxville—one of the largest stadiums in the country—becomes a sea of orange jerseys and other gear. The stadium is known for its unique checkerboard end zones and the Pride of the Southland Band forming a "T" for the team to run through.

BASKETBALL BUZZ

Tennessee is not just about American football, it's a basketball powerhouse too! The Tennessee Volunteers men's and women's teams showcase incredible talent and determination, while the Memphis Grizzlies electrify the NBA scene.

MEMPHIS GRIZZLIES

Over in Memphis, the Grizzlies rear up against their opponents on the court in the NBA (National Basketball Association). Playing at the FedExForum, the Grizzlies have become known for their "Grit and Grind" style of play, with a reputation for tough defensive play and relentless effort. The team's iconic bear logo and vibrant blue and yellow colors are a staple in the city, especially during playoff runs that ignite the whole community.

COLLEGE HOOPS

Don't forget about college basketball. The Tennessee Volunteers' men's and women's basketball teams are both top contenders. The Lady Vols, coached for decades by the legendary Pat Summitt, have a legacy of excellence with multiple national championships.

ICE HOCKEY

Did you know Tennessee is a hotbed for ice hockey? The state boasts not one, but two professional hockey teams that bring plenty of action to the ice.

NASHVILLE PREDATORS

The Nashville Predators, an NHL team established in 1998, have quickly become a staple of the Nashville sports scene. Playing home games at Bridgestone Arena, the Predators are known for their passionate fanbase, often referred to as "Smashville." A unique practice among Predators fans is the throwing of catfish onto the ice, a fun and quirky twist to the usual hockey traditions.

KNOXVILLE ICE BEARS

On the other end of the state, the Knoxville Ice Bears play in the Southern Professional Hockey League (SPHL). Established in 2002, the Ice Bears have won multiple President's Cup championships, showcasing their dominance in the league. Home games at the Knoxville Civic Coliseum are a must-see, offering affordable family-friendly entertainment and a thrilling hockey experience.

CAVING OR SPELUNKING

Caving, or spelunking, in Tennessee is an underground adventure like no other! The state is home to over 10,000 caves, making it one of the best places in the country for exploring subterranean wonders. From the massive rooms of the

Cumberland Caverns to the stunning underground waterfall at Ruby Falls, Tennessee's caves offer a thrilling experience for adventurers of all skill levels.

For those new to caving, guided tours are available at many of the popular sites, providing fascinating insights into the geology, history and wildlife of these underground marvels. Seasoned spelunkers can enjoy more challenging excursions into lesser-known caves that require crawling, climbing and squeezing through tight passages.

RODEO
Rodeo might not be the first thing that comes to mind when you think of Tennessee, but the Volunteer State has a vibrant rodeo scene that offers plenty of excitement.

Major events like the Franklin Rodeo and several International Pro Rodeo Association (IPRA) competitions bring top-tier rodeo talent to Tennessee, featuring classic events such as bull riding, barrel racing and saddle bronc riding. The state also has a strong youth rodeo scene, with organizations like the Tennessee High School Rodeo Association (THSRA) providing opportunities for young cowboys and cowgirls to compete and hone their skills.

In addition to professional and youth rodeos, Tennessee hosts ranch rodeos and smaller local events that give spectators a taste of traditional ranching activities. Venues like the Ag Expo Park in Franklin and the Nashville Fairgrounds host large-scale rodeo events, while many smaller rodeos support local charities and foster community spirit.

NASCAR RACING

NASCAR racing is a high-octane thrill ride that has a special place in Tennessee's heart. The state is home to the legendary Bristol Motor Speedway, known as "The Last Great Colosseum," where some of the most exciting and intense NASCAR races take place. With its high-banked turns and close-quarters racing, Bristol offers an adrenaline rush like no other. The Bristol Night Race, in particular, is a fan favorite, turning the speedway into a dazzling arena of speed and excitement under the lights.

For those new to the sport, NASCAR racing involves stock cars speeding around oval road tracks, with drivers competing to be the first to cross the finish line after a set number of laps. It's not just about speed—strategy, skill and endurance play huge roles. Drivers must navigate tight turns, manage tire wear and make strategic pit stops for fuel and adjustments, all while jostling for position with other racers at speeds often exceeding 200 mph. The result is a spectacle of roaring engines, precision driving and edge-of-your-seat excitement.

HUNTING

Hunting is deeply embedded in Tennessee's culture, often passed down through generations as a family tradition. Annual hunting events and competitions, along with hunter safety courses provided by the Tennessee Wildlife Resources Agency (TWRA), foster a strong sense of community among Tennessee hunters.

The diverse landscapes—from hills in the Great Smoky Mountains to expansive fields across parts of the state—offer a range of hunting opportunities. Tennessee supports a variety of game species, including deer, turkey, and waterfowl.

The state has strict wildlife management policies to ensure sustainable hunting and protect wildlife populations. Hunting licenses and tags generate revenue for the state, and many Tennessee communities benefit economically from hunting-related activities.

FISHING

Sport fishing in Tennessee is a reel-y big deal! With its abundant lakes, rivers and streams, the state is a paradise for anglers of all levels. Tennessee's waters are teeming with a variety of fish species, including bass, catfish, crappie and trout.

One of the most popular fishing spots is the Tennessee River, renowned for its trophy-sized bass and catfish. For a more serene experience, head to the Great Smoky Mountains, where you can fly fish for trout in crystal-clear mountain streams. And let's not forget Reelfoot Lake, a natural lake created by earthquakes in the early 1800s, which offers fantastic crappie fishing.

White crappie. Image by Raver Duane, U.S. Fish and Wildlife Service, Public domain, via Wikimedia Commons.

HIKING

With its diverse landscapes, from the majestic peaks of the Great Smoky Mountains to the winding paths of the Cumberland Plateau, the state is a haven for outdoor enthusiasts of all skill levels. Tennessee boasts over 1,000 miles (1,609 km) of trails, offering hikers breathtaking vistas, hidden waterfalls and encounters with diverse wildlife.

Appalachian Trail in Tennessee. Photo by ehrlif via depositphotos.com.

One of the most iconic trails is the Appalachian Trail, which stretches over 2,000 miles (3,218 km) from Georgia to Maine, with a stunning section traversing the rugged terrain of Tennessee.

For a more leisurely stroll, explore the serene trails of Radnor Lake State Park near Nashville or take in the panoramic views along the Clingmans Dome Trail in the Great Smoky Mountains. Whether you're a seasoned trekker or a novice nature lover, hiking in Tennessee promises unforgettable experiences amidst its natural splendor!

DISC GOLF

Disc golf, sometimes called "frisbee golf," is a fun and fast-growing sport in Tennessee that's perfect for enjoying the great outdoors.

Playing disc golf. Photo by jarih via depositphotos.com

It's similar to regular golf, but instead of clubs and balls, you use discs (similar to a Frisbee) and aim for metal baskets. Tennessee boasts some fantastic disc golf courses, like the renowned Harmon Hills in Fall Branch, which is often rated among the best in the country.

CORNHOLE

Playing cornhole. Image by WoodysPhotos via depositphotos.com

Cornhole, also known as bean bag toss, is a backyard game that's a big hit in Tennessee. It's a simple yet addictive game where players take turns throwing bean bags at a raised platform with a hole at the far end. The goal is to score points by landing the bag on the board or, better yet, sinking it through the hole. Tennessee's love for cornhole shines at tailgates, BBQs and family gatherings. The game's easygoing vibe makes it perfect for all ages and skill levels.

11

FAMOUS INVENTIONS MADE IN TENNESSEE

THE MINIATURE GOLF COURSE: A HOLE-IN-ONE INVENTION

In the late 1920s, Garnet Carter, a resident of Lookout Mountain, Tennessee, introduced the world to miniature golf. Inspired by the desire to entertain guests at his hotel, Carter built a small-scale golf course on his property, complete with obstacles and challenges. He called it "Tom Thumb Golf," after the famous fictional character.

Carter's miniature golf course was an instant success, attracting visitors from far and wide. In fact, it's said that even President Warren G. Harding played a round of miniature golf on Carter's course during a visit to Lookout Mountain. Today, miniature golf courses can be found in nearly every corner of the globe, providing hours of fun for families and friends.

THE TOW-TRUCK

A tow truck, also known as a wrecker, recovery vehicle, or breakdown lorry, has long been used to move or recover disabled vehicles. The invention of the first tow truck is credited to Ernest Holmes, Sr., a mechanic from Chattanooga, Tennessee, who created it in 1916.

Holmes's invention came about after he had to use blocks, ropes and six men to pull a car out of a creek. This incident sparked his idea for a better solution. It led to the development of the Holmes Wrecker, a towing apparatus mounted on the back of a vehicle that featured a twin boom wrecker with lifting jib, revolutionizing roadside assistance.

TYPEWRITER RIBBON
The invention of the typewriter ribbon is attributed to several individuals and companies over time, and its development took place in various locations. However, Memphis resident George K. Anderson secured a patent for "new and useful improvements in typewriter ribbon" in 1886. Anderson's patent focused on advancements in the design and construction of typewriter ribbons to enhance their durability and usability.

OVERNIGHT DELIVERY
Back in the 1970s, Memphis, Tennessee, became the birthplace of a game-changing concept in the shipping industry.

Fred Smith, a college student at the time, proposed an idea for a delivery service that would transport packages overnight employing a hub-and-spoke system. Despite skepticism from industry experts, Smith's idea took flight with the founding of Federal Express (now FedEx) in 1971. This innovative approach not only transformed the way packages were delivered but also paved the way for the rapid expansion of express shipping services worldwide.

FAMILY-FRIENDLY, BUDGET ACCOMMODATION

Back in 1952, Kemmons Wilson, a Memphis native, embarked on a road trip with his family and was disappointed by the lack of quality, affordable accommodations along the way. Determined to change this, Wilson founded Holiday Inn, a chain of budget-friendly hotels offering consistent quality and service. The first Holiday Inn opened in Memphis, and its success spurred rapid expansion across the country, making affordable and comfortable lodging accessible to travelers everywhere.

One of the things he revolutionized was having a consistent experience across all of the Holiday Inn locations. He insisted that every Holiday Inn allowed children to stay for free, and included a swimming pool, free parking, air conditioning, free cribs, telephones, television and ice.

DUMPSTER

In 1935, George Dempster, an entrepreneur from Knoxville, introduced the Dempster-Dumpster. This roll-out revolutionized how we handle waste. Initially designed for Dempster's construction company, this innovative waste container featured a hinged lid, and wheels for mobility. It quickly gained popularity, becoming essential in waste management practices worldwide. Today, the term "Dumpster" is universally recognized, a testament to George Dempster's Tennessee ingenuity.

DID YOU KNOW?

In the UK, the term "skip" refers to a large metal container used for the temporary storage and transportation of waste materials. This device is commonly known as a "dumpster" in other parts of the world.

SELF-SERVE GROCERY STORES

Think about this: before September 6, 1916, shopping for groceries was a real chore! Shoppers would hand over a list, and the store clerk would hustle around collecting items. Talk about an oh-so inefficient time drain! But then Clarence Saunders, a true trailblazer from Memphis, had a lightbulb moment. He opened the very first Piggly Wiggly® and changed grocery-shopping forever. This wasn't just any store; it was the dawn of self-service! Customers got to stroll down aisles picking out their groceries personally. No more waiting!

Piggly Wiggly was such a hit that it sparked a shopping frenzy. It introduced features we take for granted today, such as shopping carts, price tags on every item and checkout stands. Saunders even patented his self-service store layout, setting the blueprint for modern supermarkets everywhere!

THE COTTON CANDY MACHINE

Cotton candy, also known as candy floss or fairy floss, is a sugary confection made from finely spun sugar. While the invention of cotton candy itself dates back to the late 19th century, the modern cotton candy machine, which revolutionized its production, has ties to Tennessee.

Thomas Patton, a native of Nashville, Tennessee, invented the modern cotton candy machine in 1900. Patton's machine used centrifugal force to spin sugar into fine strands, creating the fluffy texture characteristic of cotton candy. This invention made cotton candy production faster and more efficient, leading to its widespread availability at fairs, carnivals and other events.

MOON PIES

Moon pie. Photo by Evan-Amos, Public domain, via Wikimedia Commons

Back in 1917, Earl Mitchell Sr., a savvy baker at the Chattanooga Bakery in Tennessee, cooked up a real treat for the local coal miners—a snack that packed a punch for their long workdays. He created the original Moon Pie, with two graham cracker cookies and a marshmallow filling, all dipped in a delightful chocolate coating. These tasty morsels were originally quite the handful, measuring a hefty four inches (10.16 cm) in diameter. They've slimmed down over the years, but their appeal has only grown, making them a beloved Southern classic.

MOUNTAIN DEW

In the 1940s, two enterprising beverage bottlers from Knoxville, Tennessee—Barney and Ally Hartman—created Mountain Dew, a citrus-flavored soda originally designed as a whiskey mixer. The name "Mountain Dew" was a playful nod to Appalachian moonshine, reflecting the drink's rugged, outdoorsy appeal.

Over the years, Mountain Dew has been mixed with whiskey and picked up a few regional names, like the "Mountain Jack" when paired with Jack Daniel's Tennessee Whiskey and "Turkey Dew" with Wild Turkey bourbon. By 1964, the Tip Corporation took notice of its popularity and brought Mountain Dew to the national stage after PepsiCo acquired the brand.

DID YOU KNOW?
Mountain Dew's original mascot was a hillbilly character named "Willy the Hillbilly."
In the early years of Mountain Dew's marketing, "Willy the Hillbilly" was indeed featured as the mascot in advertisements and on packaging. The character reflected the beverage's Appalachian roots and its association with the region's culture.

BOTTLED COCA-COLA

While Coca-Cola syrup was invented by a pharmacist in Georgia and initially mixed and served at soda fountains, the first bottling of Coca-Cola, the drink, occurred in Tennessee. In 1899, two Chattanooga attorneys, Benjamin F. Thomas and Joseph B. Whitehead, purchased the bottling rights to the drink for $1.00, and began the process of bottling the beverage. The first bottle of Coca-Cola came off a plant on Patten Parkway in downtown Chattanooga.

This marked the beginning of the franchised bottling system for Coca-Cola. The first Coca-Cola bottling plant was established in Chattanooga, Tennessee, and it played a significant role in the expansion and distribution of Coca-Cola throughout the United States and beyond.

DID YOU KNOW?

The unique contour shape of the Coca-Cola bottle, introduced in 1916, is one of the most recognizable packaging designs in the world. Coca-Cola has trademarked the shape of its bottle to protect it from imitation by competitors. This means that other companies cannot use a similar bottle design that could potentially confuse consumers and dilute the distinctiveness of the Coca-Cola brand.

GOO GOO CLUSTER CANDY BAR

Goo Goo Cluster. Photo by Evan-Amos, Public domain, via Wikimedia Commons

Step back to 1912, when Howell Campbell Sr., a visionary from Nashville's Standard Candy Company, whipped up something extraordinary. Introducing the Goo Goo Cluster: a delightful mash-up of caramel, marshmallow nougat, fresh roasted peanuts, and covered in milk chocolate. Not just any candy, it was hailed as the first-ever combination candy bar to hit the shelves.

The name "Goo Goo" is as cute as it sounds, inspired by the babbling of a baby, hinting that this candy is so good that anyone, no matter the age, would crave it. This treat quickly stole the hearts of the South and hasn't let go. Holding true to tradition, the original Goo Goo Cluster recipe has stood the test of time, with little change over more than a century.

JACK DANIEL'S WHISKEY

Back in the 1860s, a young Jasper Newton "Jack" Daniel fired up his still in Lynchburg, Tennessee, and crafted what would become one of the world's most legendary whiskeys. Jack Daniel's Tennessee Whiskey is renowned for its distinct flavor, thanks to a unique charcoal mellowing process known as the Lincoln County Process. This technique involves filtering the whiskey through charcoal made from sugar maple wood before aging, giving it a smooth, rich taste that sets it apart from other whiskeys.

But there's more to this iconic brand. Did you know that Jack Daniel was only a teenager when he started distilling his famous whiskey? And despite its global fame, every drop of Jack Daniel's is still produced in Lynchburg, a small town with a population of just over 6,000 people. Remarkably, Lynchburg is located in a dry county, meaning the sale of alcohol is prohibited—except at the distillery itself, where you can buy a commemorative bottle or two.

KRYSTAL BURGERS

Originating in Chattanooga, Tennessee, Krystal burgers have become a Southern fast-food icon since their inception in 1932. Known for their small size and big flavor, these square-shaped, steam-grilled small sandwiches have captured the hearts and taste buds of locals and visitors alike. Paired with hot, fresh fries and a range of famous milkshakes, Krystal has become a cherished part of Tennessee's culinary landscape.

12

RANDOM AND AWESOME

THE BODY FARM

The Body Farm, officially known as the Forensic Anthropology Center at the University of Tennessee, is a one-of-a-kind research facility located in Knoxville, Tennessee. Established in 1981 by anthropologist Dr. William M. Bass, the Body Farm is dedicated to studying human decomposition under various environmental conditions.

The farm consists of outdoor laboratories, where donated human bodies are left to decompose naturally, allowing researchers the opportunity to observe and document the stages of decomposition. This research is crucial for advancing forensic science—aiding law enforcement in solving crimes, identifying human remains and providing crucial evidence in legal proceedings. The Body Farm has helped researchers improve techniques for estimating time since death and understand factors that influence decomposition.

Additionally, the Body Farm has trained countless forensic

professionals, including law enforcement officers, medical examiners and forensic scientists, making it a vital resource in the field of forensic anthropology. Though fascinating, the Body Farm is not open to visitors.

MOST POPULAR LAST NAMES IN TENNESSEE

Smith, Jones and Johnson. These are some of the most popular last names in the United States and in Tennessee. Smith is the most common last name in the U.S., and it is also the most common last name in Tennessee. Jones is the second most common last name in the U.S. and in Tennessee. Johnson is the third most common last name in the U.S. and in Tennessee.

These last names are all of English origin. Smith means "blacksmith," Jones means "son of John," and Johnson also means "son of John." These last names were originally given to people who worked in these occupations, but they have since become common surnames.

The popularity of these last names in Tennessee is likely due to the state's history. Tennessee was settled by a large number of English people, and these last names were common among the English population. Additionally, Tennessee was a major slave state, and many slaves were given the last names of their masters. As a result, these last names became even more common in the state.

CHARMING & UNCONVENTIONAL TOWN NAMES

Bugscuffle: Bugscuffle is an unincorporated community in Tennessee known for its peculiar name, which likely originated from disputes among early settlers over land or resources.

Sweet Lips: Sweet Lips is a small community in southwestern Tennessee with a charmingly unusual name that is sure to raise a few eyebrows. The name comes from Civil War times when soldiers claimed the small creek nearby was the "sweetest" they had ever tasted.

Difficult: Difficult is a small unincorporated community located in Smith County. The origin of the name is somewhat unclear, though one local legend suggests that when residents first applied for a post office, their preferred name was rejected as being "too difficult." Instead of coming up with a new name, they embraced the feedback and officially named the town "Difficult" in response.

Paris: Paris is a small town in Henry County, located in the northwestern part of the state. Founded in 1823, it was named after Paris, France, as a tribute to Marquis de Lafayette, a French aristocrat who played a key role in the American Revolution. Paris, Tennessee has its very own Eiffel Tower replica that stands at 70 feet (21 meters) high and is famous for the hosting the "World's Biggest Fish Fry."

DID YOU KNOW?

The U.S. actually has 20 different cities in 19 different states with the name Paris. Because one wasn't enough, Ohio has two in two different counties.

BODY IN THE TENNESSEE STATE CAPITOL BUILDING

Tennessee State Capitol building. Photo by Mliss via depositphotos.com

The Tennessee State Capitol, a striking example of Greek Revival architecture in Nashville, is one of architect William Strickland's crowning achievements. Strickland, who was deeply influenced by ancient Greek design, embarked on this project in 1845, aiming to create a lasting symbol of democracy and governance. However, he passed away in 1854 before its completion, and was buried within the Capitol's walls.

Guinness World Records Tied to Tennessee

WORLD'S LARGEST GAS STATION: BUC-EE'S

In the heart of Sevierville, Tennessee, you'll find the world's largest gas station. Buc-ee's is a Texas-based chain known for its super-sized convenience stores. Spanning an astonishing 74,000 square feet and featuring 120 fuel pumps, this mammoth gas station is more like a roadside attraction than a mere pit stop.

Beyond its impressive size, Buc-ee's offers a wide array of amenities, including freshly made barbecue, a bakery with irresistible treats, a vast selection of snacks and even a shopping area filled with strange souvenirs and local crafts.

WORLD'S LARGEST CEDAR BUCKET

Nestled in Murfreesboro, Tennessee, stands an extraordinary and quirky attraction—the world's largest cedar bucket. Originally crafted in 1887 by the Tennessee Red Cedar Woodenworks Company, this colossal bucket measures an impressive 6 feet (1.8 meters) tall and 5.5 feet (1.6 meters) in diameter, with a capacity to hold over 1,500 gallons (5,678 liters) of water. To put this into perspective, this is roughly half the volume of a Concrete Mixer Truck that holds about 2,900 gallons (10,977 liters).

The bucket was initially created as a marketing tool, to showcase the company's craftsmanship and the durability of Tennessee cedar. Though it suffered damage over the years, it was meticulously reconstructed and now proudly resides at Cannonsburgh Village, a historic pioneer village.

WORLD'S LARGEST FIREWORK STORE

It turns out that the world's largest firework store is indeed located just outside of Knoxville, Tennessee. The Fireworks Supermarket in Knoxville holds this impressive title, offering an expansive selection of fireworks across its vast showroom. This giant store is designed to be a high-end shopping experience for fireworks enthusiasts, providing everything from sparklers to elaborate aerial displays, all under one roof.

In Tennessee, you must be at least 16 years old to purchase fireworks, and they can only be purchased during specific times of the year—June 20 to July 5 or December 10 to January 2.

WORLD'S LARGEST RUBIK'S CUBE

In the heart of Knoxville, Tennessee, you can find the world's largest Rubik's Cube, a striking relic from the 1982 World's Fair. This massive puzzle, standing 10 feet (3 meters) tall and weighing 1,200 pounds (544 kg), originally greeted visitors at the entrance to the Hungarian Pavilion during the fair.

The cube, now housed in the Knoxville Convention Center, features hidden motors that allow it to rotate and change color patterns, captivating onlookers with its impressive size and intricate design.

WORLD'S LARGEST FISH FRY

Every year, Paris, Tennessee, hosts the World's Largest Fish Fry, a week-long celebration that attracts thousands of visitors. Starting as a small gathering in 1953, the event has grown to feature over 12,500 pounds (5,670 kg) of catfish served annually. A classic fish fry includes all-you-can-eat fried catfish with Southern sides like hushpuppies, coleslaw, and fries, creating a friendly, down-home dining experience.

Held during the last full week of April, the event centers around the Robert E. "Bobby" Cox Memorial Fish Tent and includes parades, a carnival, rodeos, beauty pageants, and even catfish races, making it a true Tennessee tradition.

WORLD'S LONGEST MULLET

In Knoxville, Tennessee, Tami Manis holds the Guinness World Record for the world's longest competitive female mullet. Measuring an astonishing 5 feet 8 inches (172.72 cm), Tami's mullet is even longer than she is tall!

Tami Manis, World Record holder for World's longest mullet. Photo courtesy of Tami Manis.

She began growing her hair in 1990 after being inspired by the music video for "Voices Carry" by 'Til Tuesday.

Over the years, her impressive mullet has become a local legend and a conversation starter, with friends and strangers alike marveling at its length.

THE WORLD'S TALLEST TREEHOUSE

For more than 25 years, the world's tallest treehouse could be found about 100-miles (160.9 km) east of Nashville in the town of Crossville. Built in the early 1990's by Horace Burgess, a minister and landscaper, it became a major tourist attraction. It took over 11 years to build, used over 258,000 nails and had 80 rooms over five floors. It was constructed around an 80-foot (24.38 m) tall White Oak tree. Unfortunately, a mysterious fire burned the impressive 97-foot (29.56 m) structure down in 2019.

YOU KNOW YOU'RE IN TENNESSEE WHEN...

You know you're in Tennessee when...

"You find yourself having a passionate debate about the best BBQ style."

You know you're in Tennessee when...

"The tea is sweet enough to make your dentist wince, and you wouldn't have it any other way."

You know you're in Tennessee when...

"Every other car has a University of Tennessee sticker, and it's perfectly normal to wear orange on game day."

You know you're in Tennessee when...

"You've got a choice of live music venues every night of the week, and none of them play the same genre."

You know you're in Tennessee when…

"You can't drive five miles without seeing a historic marker or a Civil War battlefield."

You know you're in Tennessee when…

"You start measuring distance in hours, not miles—'It's about two hours from Nashville.'"

You know you're in Tennessee when…

"You find yourself at a festival dedicated to a fruit, vegetable or grain almost every other weekend."

You know you're in Tennessee when…

"Your idea of a traffic jam is getting stuck behind a tractor on a country road."

You know you're in Tennessee when…

"Hearing 'Rocky Top' makes you automatically respond with a 'Woo!'"

You know you're in Tennessee when…

"Strangers smile and say 'hello' on the street, and it doesn't feel weird at all."

You know you're in Tennessee when…

"You plan your autumn around a visit to the Smokies to see the leaves change."

You know you're in Tennessee when…

"There's a church on nearly every corner, and each one claims to have the best potluck dinners."

14

FUN FOOD AND DRINK FACTS

OFFICIAL STATE BEVERAGE: MILK
While Tennessee is famous for its Tennessee Whiskey, it's milk that holds the official state beverage title. Tennessee has a strong dairy farming legacy, with a history dating back to early settlers.

The state produces millions of gallons of milk annually. Tennessee's dairy industry also produces a diverse range of dairy products, including cheese, yogurt and ice cream. Institutions like the University of Tennessee Institute of Agriculture support dairy education and research, while many farmers participate in the farm-to-table movement, providing fresh milk and dairy products directly to consumers.

TENNESSEE WHISKEY
Tennessee whiskey isn't just a drink; it's a whole experience. Known for its smooth taste and unique distilling process, this iconic spirit has put Tennessee on the map for whiskey lovers around the world.

Jack Daniel's: Lynchburg is home to the world-famous Jack Daniel's Distillery, the oldest registered distillery in the U.S. Founded in 1866, Jack Daniel's is known for its signature Old No. 7, which has become a global symbol of quality Tennessee whiskey. The distillery offers tours where you can see the whole process, from charcoal mellowing to bottling, and of course, sample some of their best offerings.

George Dickel: Another big name in Tennessee whiskey is George Dickel, located in Tullahoma. George Dickel prides itself on its traditional craftsmanship, using the same methods since the 1800s. They even spell "whisky" without the "e" to honor the Scottish tradition. Their Cascade Hollow Distilling Co. offers tours that give you a peek into their meticulous process, and provide a taste of their smooth, mellow whisky.

The Lincoln County Process: What sets Tennessee whiskey apart from bourbon is the Lincoln County Process. This involves filtering the whiskey through charcoal before aging, giving it a smoother flavor. This method is a requirement for any whiskey to be officially labeled as Tennessee whiskey.

Whiskey and Culture: Tennessee whiskey isn't just about the drink; it's a big part of the state's culture. Many distilleries host events, festivals and tastings that draw visitors from all over. It's a great way to experience Southern hospitality and the rich history of whiskey-making.

MEMPHIS-STYLE BBQ

Memphis is a BBQ lover's paradise. Whether you're into dry rub or saucy ribs, the city's got plenty of joints—such as the famous Rendezvous, or Central BBQ—where you can get your fix.

For a true Memphis pulled pork experience, the coleslaw goes on top of the pulled pork in the sandwich, rather than eaten as a side dish.

NASHVILLE HOT CHICKEN

Spicy Nashville hot chicken sandwich with pickles and coleslaw. Photo by Resnick_joshua1 via depositphotos.com

This spicy fried chicken dish is a Nashville original. It's spicy, crispy, and totally worth the heat. Prince's Hot Chicken Shack is credited with its creation. The chicken is marinated in buttermilk, breaded, and fried until crispy. It's then doused in a cayenne pepper-based sauce that gives the dish its signature heat. To help balance the spice, it's commonly served with pickles and white bread.

The legend of Nashville's hot chicken traces back to Thornton Prince, a charismatic figure known for his love of nightlife and fried chicken.

During the Great Depression, Prince's romantic escapades earned him a reputation, much to the chagrin of his steady girlfriend. Seeking revenge, she concocted a spicy fried chicken recipe, hoping to teach him a lesson. However, to her surprise, Prince not only enjoyed the fiery dish but also perfected the recipe, leading to the birth of hot chicken. Prince's Hot Chicken Shack became a beloved institution in Nashville, with his great niece, Ms. Andre Prince Jeffries, carrying on the tradition today.

Despite the trend's widespread popularity, Prince's Hot Chicken remains the original and continues to set the standard for hot chicken in the South.

FRIED PIES

Fried pies are a cherished part of Tennessee's culinary landscape. These deliciously indulgent treats have been enjoyed for generations. The handheld pies are made by enclosing a sweet or savory filling in buttermilk pastry dough and frying until golden and crispy. They are a popular choice for snacks, desserts or a quick meal on the go. What sets Tennessee's fried pies apart is their wide range of fillings, from classic fruit flavors like apple and peach to regional favorites like sweet potato or barbecue pork.

FRIED GREEN TOMATOES

Fried Green Tomatoes with sauce. Photo by bhofack2 via depositphotos.com

Fried green tomatoes are more than just a delicious dish—they're a symbol of resilience and adaptation in Southern culinary culture. Born out of necessity during times of hardship, such as the Great Depression, fried green tomatoes showcase the resourcefulness of Southern cooks, who found creative ways to utilize unripe tomatoes that would otherwise go to waste.

COUNTRY HAM

While country ham isn't exclusive to Tennessee, you'll find it on many Tennessee menus. Country ham is salt-cured and aged for an extended period, often several months or even up to a year. This is what gives it a distinctively salty and savory flavor.

STACK CAKE AKA TENNESSEE MOUNTAIN CAKE

Stack Cake, also known as Tennessee Mountain Cake, is a traditional Appalachian dessert. This unique cake consists of multiple thin layers of cake shaped from dough, rather than batter, and baked without a cake pan, resulting in dry and brittle layers reminiscent of large cookies. Between each layer the cake has a sweet filling, such as apple butter or dried fruit, adding moisture and flavor to the cake.

Originally served at weddings and special occasions in rural Appalachian communities, Stack Cake is a symbol of community and togetherness. Often, each layer is made by a different family member or neighbor. After assembly, the cake is wrapped in plastic and refrigerated overnight, allowing the flavors to meld together for a deliciously moist and flavorful final product.

CORNBREAD

This beloved staple is enjoyed in various forms across the state, from classic skillet cornbread to cornbread muffins and cornbread sticks. Tennessee's cornbread is often made with a mix of cornmeal, flour, eggs, buttermilk and baking powder, resulting in a moist and flavorful texture.

Additionally, Tennessee's cornbread can be either "sweet" or "savory," with some recipes incorporating ingredients like sugar, honey or even bacon grease for added richness.

Cornbread has a long history in Tennessee, dating back to Native American cultures who first cultivated maize in the region.

DID YOU KNOW?

There's an annual celebration for all things cornbread at the National Cornbread Festival in South Pittsburg, Tennessee. Held in late April, the festival serves as a platform to showcase the culinary talents of local chefs and home cooks, as well as the rich cultural heritage of Tennessee's cornbread tradition.

BAKED BEANS

When it comes to Southern barbecues and family gatherings in Tennessee, baked beans are a beloved staple. This hearty side dish, often simmered with a rich blend of brown sugar, molasses, onions and bacon perfectly complements the smoky flavors of Tennessee barbecue. Each family or barbecue joint might have its own secret recipe, handed down through generations, making every pot of baked beans an irreplaceable culinary treasure.

DID YOU KNOW?

In the UK, baked beans have a unique place in the cuisine! Unlike in the U.S., where they're a barbecue side, Brits often enjoy baked beans as part of a traditional breakfast, served over toast with a sprinkle of salt and pepper.

They're also a common component of the famous "full English breakfast," alongside eggs, sausages, and other hearty items.

TENNESSEE'S BUSH'S BAKED BEANS

Nestled in the foothills of the Great Smoky Mountains, Bush Brothers & Company has been a Tennessee treasure since 1908. While many know Bush's Baked Beans for their iconic commercials featuring Duke the dog, few realize that the original family recipe hails from Chestnut Hill, Tennessee. The secret family recipe, guarded closely for over a century, combines tender navy beans with a rich, savory sauce, creating a taste beloved by millions.

Visitors to the area can even explore the Bush's Visitor Center, where they can learn about the company's history, see the canning process and enjoy a meal at the on-site café.

FRIED PICKLES

Fried pickles are a beloved Southern delicacy, especially in Tennessee. This crispy and tangy treat consists of pickle slices that are coated in a seasoned batter, then deep-fried to golden perfection. Often eaten alongside a plate of BBQ or enjoyed as a crunchy snack served with a variety of dipping sauces.

FUDGE PIE

Fudge pie is a rich, chocolatey delight that combines the gooey texture of a brownie with the flaky crust of a pie, creating a perfect harmony of flavors and textures.

Originating in the South, fudge pie became especially popular in Tennessee, where recipes have been handed down through generations. Today, fudge pie continues to be a beloved dessert at family gatherings, holiday feasts, and local diners.

BANANA PUDDIN'

Individual portions of banana puddin'. Photo by aliced via depositphotos.com

In Tennessee, no Southern meal is complete without a serving of banana pudding, or "banana puddin'," as locals lovingly call it. This classic dessert layers vanilla wafers, ripe bananas and creamy vanilla pudding, all topped with a fluffy meringue or whipped cream. Banana pudding has become a cherished part of family gatherings, church potlucks and barbecue feasts across the state. The recipe often varies, with some families adding their own special twists, like caramel drizzle or a hint of bourbon.

The earliest known recipe for banana pudding appeared in the late 19th century. However, it wasn't until the 1940s that Nabisco began printing their recipe on vanilla wafer boxes, which helped popularize the dish nationwide.

BISCUITS AND GRAVY

Biscuits and gravy. Photo by Resnick_joshua1 via depositphotos.com

In Tennessee, biscuits and gravy are the epitome of Southern comfort food. Fluffy, buttery biscuits smothered in rich, creamy sausage gravy create a hearty breakfast that's hard to beat. This beloved dish has humble beginnings, originally served as a filling meal for hardworking farmers and laborers.

While sausage gravy is the most common, there are regional variations across the South. In Tennessee, you might find biscuits topped with red-eye gravy, made from country ham drippings and coffee, or even chocolate gravy, a sweet treat that's particularly popular in Appalachian regions.

RAMPS OR WILD LEEKS

Wild leeks, affectionately known as ramps, are a cherished springtime delicacy in Tennessee. These pungent, garlicky greens grow wild in the Appalachian forests and are foraged by locals who eagerly await their brief season each year. Ramps have been a staple in Appalachian cuisine for centuries, often used in traditional dishes like ramp soup, ramp pesto, and scrambled eggs with ramps.

Ramps were once considered a medicinal herb by Native American tribes, who used them to treat colds and other ailments. Today, ramps are celebrated at annual festivals, such as the Cosby Ramp Festival in Tennessee, where locals and visitors alike can enjoy this unique, flavorful ingredient.

SWEET ICED TEA

Sweet Iced Tea with lemon. Photo by TeriVirbickis via depositphotos.com

In Tennessee, sweet iced tea isn't just a drink, it's a way of life. Approximately 85% of all tea consumed in America is iced tea. And a significant portion of that is sweet tea, especially in the South.

Made by brewing strong black tea and sweetening it generously with one to two cups of sugar per gallon (about 200 to 400 grams of sugar per 3.78 liters), sweet tea is often enhanced with a slice of lemon or a sprig of mint for that Southern flair.

Dating back to the early 19th century when tea and sugar were luxury items, sweet tea has deep roots. The oldest known recipe was published in 1879 in "Housekeeping in Old Virginia" by Marion Cabell Tyree.

Today, Tennessee's love for sweet tea remains unwavering, with many locals passing down their special recipes through generations. Whether served in mason jars or tall glasses, sweet iced tea is a staple at family gatherings, barbecues and front porch sittin', offering the perfect antidote to the hot Southern sun and symbolizing warm hospitality.

15

INTERESTING WAR HISTORY

REVOLUTIONARY WAR & THE OVERMOUNTAIN MEN (1775–1783)
Tennessee's early settlers played a significant role in the American Revolutionary War. The Overmountain Men, a group of frontier militia, marched from what is now eastern Tennessee to fight in the Battle of Kings Mountain in 1780. This crucial victory helped turn the tide against British forces in the Southern campaign.

THE WAR OF 1812 (1812–1815)
The War of 1812 was fought between the United States and the British Empire, with Tennessee playing a significant role. Tennesseans volunteered in large numbers, earning the state its nickname, "The Volunteer State." Under the leadership of General Andrew Jackson, Tennessee volunteers played crucial roles in the Creek War (part of the larger conflict) and the decisive Battle of New Orleans. These battles helped secure American control over the Mississippi Territory and boosted national morale.

ANDREW JACKSON & THE BATTLE OF NEW ORLEANS

Before he became the seventh President of the United States, Andrew Jackson was a war hero from Tennessee. He led American forces to a decisive victory against the British in the Battle of New Orleans during the War of 1812. Despite being outnumbered, Jackson's troops managed to secure a significant win, making Jackson a household name.

TENNESSEE IN THE SPANISH-AMERICAN WAR (1898)

During the Spanish-American War in 1898, the USS Nashville, a gunboat named after Tennessee's capital, made history by firing the first American shot of the conflict. The ship's crew captured a Spanish vessel off the coast of Cuba, marking the start of the war. This unexpected connection underscores Tennessee's impact on American naval history—even as a landlocked state.

TENNESSEE'S NICKNAME: THE VOLUNTEER STATE

Tennessee earned its nickname, "The Volunteer State," during the War of 1812 when thousands of Tennesseans volunteered to fight. This reputation was cemented during the Mexican-American War, where an overwhelming number of volunteers from Tennessee answered the call to arms. Their bravery and commitment are still celebrated today.

THE CIVIL WAR (1861–1865): CIVIL WAR HOTSPOT

Tennessee's rivers and railroads were vital for both Confederate and Union forces during the Civil War, leading to intense battles for control over these critical transportation routes. Notably, the Battle of Shiloh, fought in April 1862, was one of the war's bloodiest battles, with over 23,000 casualties. The state witnessed numerous significant battles, including those at Fort Donelson, Chattanooga and Nashville.

THE TENNESSEE MOUNTED INFANTRY

Tennessee contributed a distinct regiment known as the Tennessee Mounted Infantry during the Civil War. These troops, adept at using both horses and rifles, were highly mobile and effective in guerrilla warfare tactics, making them a formidable force.

TENNESSEE'S OWN IRONCLAD

The Confederate ironclad warship, the CSS Tennessee, played a significant role in the Civil War. It participated in the Battle of Mobile Bay in 1864, demonstrating Tennessee's naval engineering prowess despite its eventual capture by Union forces.

CONFEDERATE SUBMARINE PIONEER

Tennessee native Horace Lawson Hunley was a pioneer in submarine design during the Civil War. He designed the H.L. Hunley, the first combat submarine to sink an enemy warship. Though Hunley died during a test run, his invention marked a significant advancement in naval warfare.

THE BATTLE OF FRANKLIN

The Battle of Franklin, fought on November 30, 1864, was one of the fiercest battles of the Civil War. Confederate forces launched a massive assault against fortified Union positions, resulting in heavy casualties, including the deaths of six Confederate generals. Today, the battlefield is preserved as a historic site.

NICKNAMED THE BUTTERNUTS
Tennessee soldiers and their Confederate comrades were nicknamed "Butternuts" due to their uniforms' tan color, dyed using butternut tree nuts. This nickname symbolized their Southern roots and distinctive appearance.

THE LAST AND THE FIRST
During the Civil War, Tennessee was the last state to secede from the Union in 1861 and the first to be readmitted after the war in 1866.

GREENVILLE'S UNIQUE MONUMENTS FOR EACH SIDE
In Greeneville, Tennessee's second oldest town, two monuments stand on the lawn of the Greene County Courthouse. On one side is a monument honoring soldiers who enlisted in the Union Army and on the other side a monument honoring a Confederate General. This is the only place in the U.S. that honors both Union and Confederate soldiers, symbolizing Greeneville's efforts to bridge the gap between the two sides of the Civil War.

THE RECONSTRUCTION ERA (1865-1877)
After the Civil War ended in 1865, the U.S. entered the Reconstruction Era (1865-1877), a time focused on rebuilding the South and establishing rights for formerly enslaved Black Americans.

During this period, Congress passed the 13th, 14th, and 15th Amendments, abolishing slavery, granting citizenship, and protecting Black men's voting rights. For the first time, Black men held public office in the South, and initiatives like the Freedmen's Bureau supported newly freed individuals with education and legal aid.

However, resistance to Reconstruction led to the rise of violent groups like the Ku Klux Klan, and the end of federal enforcement in 1877 allowed Southern states to pass Jim Crow laws, enforcing racial segregation for decades.

Tennessee & World War I (1914-1918)

FISK JUBILEE SINGERS' WAR EFFORTS
During World War I, the Fisk Jubilee Singers from Nashville's Fisk University played a significant role in supporting the war effort. They toured extensively to raise money for war bonds, using their concerts to promote African American culture and contributions at a critical time in history. Their efforts helped finance the war and brought attention to the talents and patriotism of African Americans.

OLD HICKORY: A WARTIME INDUSTRIAL HUB
In 1918, the federal government authorized the construction of a massive gunpowder factory in a small town in Tennessee that was originally called Jacksonville to honor Andrew Jackson. It was later renamed to Old Hickory, again in honor of Andrew Jackson. At its peak, this facility produced 700,000 pounds (317,514 kg) of smokeless powder per day. This enormous output was vital for supplying the U.S. military and its allies during the war.

After the war, DuPont bought the factory and it became a significant industrial employer in Middle Tennessee.

NAVAL AIR STATION MEMPHIS

During World War I, the Department of War established a military aviation school near Memphis, which became known as Park Field. Thousands of U.S. aviators were trained there, learning to fly the Curtiss JN-4 Jennys. These were an iconic biplane that became one of the most famous American training aircraft during World War I.

This facility was crucial for training military personnel and later evolved into Naval Air Station Memphis, playing an ongoing role in military aviation training and support.

ALVIN YORK: A WWI HERO FROM TENNESSEE

One of the most famous American heroes of World War I, Alvin C. York, hailed from Pall Mall, Tennessee. He was drafted into the army in 1917. Initially a conscientious objector due to his pacifist beliefs, York's views changed after discussions with his superiors and he agreed to fight. He eventually became one of the most decorated soldiers of the war.

During the Meuse-Argonne Offensive in 1918, York led a charge against German machine-gun nests, capturing 132 enemy soldiers and killing several others despite overwhelming odds. For his bravery, he was awarded the Medal of Honor and became a national hero. His life story was later immortalized in the 1941 film "Sergeant York," starring Gary Cooper.

Tennessee & World War II (1939–1945)

CAMP FORREST'S ROLE IN WWII
During WWII, Tennessee was home to several prisoner-of-war (POW) camps, including Camp Forrest near Tullahoma. This camp housed German and Italian prisoners who were treated according to Geneva Convention standards, with many opportunities to work in agriculture and local industries, contributing to the community's economy.

Life at Camp Forrest included recreational activities; some prisoners formed orchestras, played sports, and even published newspapers, creating a relatively supportive environment despite the circumstances of war.

THE MANHATTAN PROJECT & THE SECRET CITY OF OAK RIDGE
The Manhattan Project was a top-secret U.S. initiative during World War II, aimed to develop the first atomic bomb.

Oak Ridge, Tennessee, was a secret city that was established in 1942 and created from scratch as part of the Project. The city was built to house workers and scientists developing the atomic bomb. At its peak, Oak Ridge had a population of 75,000, making it one of the largest and most secretive cities in the U.S.

It was here that uranium-235 was produced for the bomb dropped on Hiroshima. Oak Ridge's contribution was vital to ending the war in the Pacific.

CLINTON ENGINEER WORKS

The official name for the Oak Ridge facilities during World War II was the Clinton Engineer Works (CEW). It included the K-25 gaseous diffusion plant, the Y-12 electromagnetic separation plant, and the X-10 Graphite Reactor, crucial in producing enriched uranium for the first atomic bombs.

Shift change at the Y-12 uranium enrichment facility in Oak Ridge, Tennessee, during the Manhattan Project. Photo by Ed Westcott / American Museum of Science and Energy, Public Domain, 1945.

WOMEN OF OAK RIDGE

Women played significant roles in Oak Ridge, working as chemists, physicists and technicians. Their contributions were vital to the Manhattan Project's success.

SECURITY AND SECRECY

Oak Ridge was shrouded in secrecy during its operation. The city was not even on official maps, and residents were restricted in their communication with the outside world. Security was tight, with guards stationed at every entrance, and workers were often kept in the dark about the overall purpose of their tasks to maintain confidentiality.

FIRST PEACETIME NUCLEAR REACTOR

After the war, the X-10 Graphite Reactor at Oak Ridge became the first reactor in the world to produce usable electricity in 1948. It marked the transition of nuclear technology from wartime applications to peacetime uses, paving the way for the development of nuclear power.

OAK RIDGE AND THE NOBEL PRIZE

In 1945, the Nobel Prize in Physics was awarded to James Chadwick for his discovery of the neutron, a particle in the nucleus of an atom. While Chadwick was not directly involved in the Manhattan Project, his discovery was fundamental to nuclear fission. Many of the scientists at Oak Ridge were inspired by his work, and the site's research contributed to several future Nobel Prize-winning discoveries.

THE CALUTRON GIRLS

A group of young women, known as the "Calutron Girls," operated the electromagnetic separation machines called calutrons at Oak Ridge.

Calutron operators at their panels, in the Y-12 plant at Oak Ridge, TN during World War II. Photo by Ed Westcott / American Museum of Science and Energy, Public Domain, circa 1943 to 54.

These women were recruited straight out of high school and trained to monitor the machines' dials and gauges. Their work was so precise that, despite not fully understanding the process, they outperformed some of the top physicists who initially operated the calutrons.

POST-WAR TRANSITION

After World War II, Oak Ridge transitioned from a military to a civilian research center. The city became home to the Oak Ridge National Laboratory (ORNL), which continues to be a leading institution in scientific research and innovation. ORNL has made significant advancements in fields such as nuclear energy, materials science and environmental studies.

THE SECRET IS OUT

The existence of Oak Ridge and its purpose remained a closely guarded secret until the end of World War II. It wasn't until the bombing of Hiroshima that the residents of Oak Ridge fully understood the impact of their work. The city's contributions to the war effort were finally revealed, earning it the nickname "The Secret City."

HISTORICAL LANDMARKS

Today, Oak Ridge is home to several historical landmarks that commemorate its role in the Manhattan Project. The American Museum of Science and Energy offers exhibits on the history and science of Oak Ridge, and the Oak Ridge International Friendship Bell symbolizes peace and the city's global impact. Visitors can also tour the X-10 Graphite Reactor, a National Historic Landmark.

EDUCATION AND OUTREACH

Oak Ridge continues to contribute to scientific education and outreach. The city hosts numerous conferences, workshops and educational programs aimed at inspiring future generations of scientists and engineers. The legacy of Oak Ridge as a center of innovation and discovery remains strong, reflecting its pivotal role in shaping modern science and technology.

WOMEN AT WAR: CONTRIBUTIONS FROM TENNESSEE

Tennessee women have a long history of involvement in wartime efforts, playing crucial roles during both World War I and World War II. They served as nurses, factory workers and even pilots. The Women Airforce Service Pilots (WASP) program included several Tennesseans who flew military aircraft to support the war effort, breaking barriers and setting precedents for future generations.

Additionally, Tennessee played a significant role in the Women's Army Corps (WAC) during World War II. Fort Oglethorpe, located just across the state line in Georgia but close to Chattanooga, was one of the primary training centers for WACs.

These women served in various capacities, from administrative roles to mechanics, breaking gender barriers and paving the way for future generations of women in the military. Their contributions were vital to the war effort and helped to shift societal perceptions of women's capabilities in traditionally male-dominated fields.

TENNESSEE'S HISTORY OF SLAVERY AND CIVIL RIGHTS

Acknowledging Hard Truths
While this book is filled with fun and fascinating facts about Tennessee, some readers have asked that I also address the state's difficult history. As a white author, I recognize that I bring my own perspective to this book and aim to respectfully touch on some of the painful but important parts of Tennessee's past, especially in relation to slavery and the civil rights movement. This is by no means a complete account—just a brief look at these histories. I hope it provides space for reflection and honors the resilience, courage, and contributions of those who fought for freedom, justice, and equality.

SLAVERY IN TENNESSEE

Tennessee's involvement with slavery began in its earliest days, with enslaved African Americans forced to work primarily in agriculture. Unlike some neighboring Southern states, Tennessee's geography led to a more varied economy, so slavery was especially concentrated in West Tennessee, where cotton plantations dominated. In contrast, East Tennessee had fewer large plantations and, before the Civil War, was known for its strong anti-slavery sentiment.

THE NASHVILLE SLAVE MARKET

Before the Civil War, Nashville was a hub for the domestic slave trade, with a prominent auction site near what is now the Morris Memorial Building. Here, enslaved individuals were routinely bought and sold, their labor enriching local traders and landowners. Today, historical markers in Nashville commemorate these painful events, encouraging visitors to reflect on the lives impacted by the trade.

TENNESSEE'S SLAVE-TRADING NETWORKS

Tennessee played a significant role in the broader U.S. slave trade, particularly in Nashville and Memphis. Firms like Bolton, Dickins & Company purchased enslaved people from the Upper South and transported them to meet high labor demand in states like Mississippi and Louisiana. Often, enslaved individuals were marched in "coffles," or chained groups, to distant plantations. This interstate trade marked a brutal reality for thousands forcibly relocated across the South.

THE RECONSTRUCTION ERA (1865-1877)

The Reconstruction Era was the period immediately following the American Civil War, lasting from 1865 to 1877. During this time, the United States focused on rebuilding the Southern states, which had been devastated by the war, and reintegrating them into the Union. This era also aimed to address the status and rights of formerly enslaved Black Americans.

Key elements of Reconstruction included:

- **Amendments to the Constitution**: The 13th, 14th, and 15th Amendments were passed during this time, abolishing slavery, granting citizenship to anyone born in the U.S., and protecting the voting rights of Black men.
- **Freedmen's Bureau**: This organization helped formerly enslaved people transition to freedom by providing education, food, and legal support.
- **Black Political Representation**: For the first time, Black men held public office in the South, with many serving in state legislatures, and some even in the U.S. Congress.

However, significant resistance arose as white Southerners opposed Reconstruction's progress, and violent groups like the Ku Klux Klan used intimidation to undermine Black rights. When the federal government withdrew troops in 1877, this effectively ended Reconstruction, opening the door to Jim Crow laws that enforced racial segregation for decades.

IDA B. WELLS & ANTI-LYNCHING ADVOCACY

Although born in Mississippi, journalist and activist Ida B. Wells made a lasting impact in Memphis, Tennessee. In 1892, three Black men—friends of Wells—were brutally lynched in Memphis after opening a grocery store that competed with a white-owned business.

This horrifying incident deeply affected Wells, inspiring her to investigate and expose the practice of lynching across the United States. She documented cases, interviewed witnesses, and uncovered that lynchings were often used to suppress Black economic success, not simply as "punishments" for alleged crimes, as was widely claimed.

Wells published her findings in Memphis newspapers and later in *The Red Record*, a groundbreaking pamphlet documenting the brutality and frequency of lynchings. Her fearless journalism made her a target, and white mobs threatened her life, eventually destroying her newspaper office.

Forced to leave Memphis, Wells continued her anti-lynching advocacy, speaking across the U.S. and Europe to raise awareness and galvanize opposition. Her work laid the foundation for future civil rights efforts and brought international attention to America's racial violence.

Is Lynching Still a Concern?

While lynching no longer occurs as it did during Wells's time, the history of racial violence and injustice has left a lasting impact. In response to this history, Tennessee and other states have taken steps to formally denounce lynching, and in 2022, Congress passed the Emmett Till Anti-Lynching Act, making lynching a federal hate crime.

CLINTON HIGH SCHOOL INTEGRATION

In 1954, the U.S. Supreme Court issued the landmark Brown v. Board of Education ruling, declaring racial segregation in public schools unconstitutional. This decision overturned the "separate but equal" doctrine established in *Plessy v. Ferguson* and called for the integration of public schools nationwide.

However, the ruling faced massive resistance in the South, including in Tennessee.

In 1956, Clinton High School in Anderson County became one of the first public schools in the South to integrate. Twelve Black students, known as the Clinton Twelve, enrolled under federal orders and faced violent protests, harassment, and community turmoil.

Despite threats and hostility, the Clinton Twelve remained steadfast, and with support from activists and federal authorities, they helped pave the way for school desegregation in Tennessee, marking a pivotal moment in the state's history.

MEMPHIS SANITATION WORKERS' STRIKE
In 1968, Memphis sanitation workers—predominantly Black—organized a strike for safer working conditions and better pay, protesting the dangerous and discriminatory treatment they endured.

Their protest gained national attention when Dr. Martin Luther King Jr. joined their efforts, delivering his famous "I've Been to the Mountaintop" speech in Memphis the night before his assassination.

This protest emphasized the deep connection between civil rights and economic justice, as workers sought fair treatment and safe working conditions. King's involvement underscored the strike's importance and brought the fight for justice in Memphis to the forefront of national attention.

HIGHLANDER FOLK SCHOOL

Founded in 1932 in Monteagle, Tennessee, the Highlander Folk School was a training ground for many civil rights activists. Leaders like **Rosa Parks** and **Dr. Martin Luther King Jr.** attended workshops there on nonviolent protest and organizing tactics.

THE NASHVILLE STUDENT MOVEMENT AND SIT-INS

In 1960, Nashville became a pivotal city in the civil rights movement as students from Fisk University, Tennessee State University, and other local colleges organized the Nashville Student Movement to challenge segregation.

Led by activists like **Diane Nash**, **James Lawson**, and **John Lewis**, the students held peaceful sit-ins at segregated lunch counters, making Nashville one of the first Southern cities to desegregate public facilities successfully.

17

MOVIES FILMED IN TENNESSEE

42 (2013)
A biographical sports drama about the groundbreaking career of baseball legend Jackie Robinson. Set in the 1940s, the film follows Robinson's journey with the Brooklyn Dodgers, as he becomes the first African American player to break the color barrier in Major League Baseball. The film includes scenes shot in Chattanooga, Tennessee, where the historic Engel Stadium was used as a filming location.

Fun Fact: To honor Jackie Robinson's significant contributions to the sport, baseball commissioner Bud Selig universally retired Robinson's jersey number 42 across all Major League Baseball teams in 1997.

COAL MINER'S DAUGHTER (1980)
This biographical film tells the story of country music legend Loretta Lynn's rise to fame from her humble beginnings in Butcher Hollow, Kentucky. The movie depicts her journey from a poverty-stricken childhood to becoming one of the most

celebrated singers in country music history. It was partially filmed on location in Tennessee, including scenes shot at the Ryman Auditorium in Nashville.

Fun Fact: Sissy Spacek did her own singing in the film. She won an Oscar for her performance as Loretta. To prepare for her role, Spacek accompanied Lynn on one of her tours, to better understand her on- and off-stage mannerisms.

THE BLIND SIDE (2009)

A heartwarming biographical film based on the true story of Michael Oher, a homeless and traumatized boy who becomes an All-American football player with the help of the Tuohy family. "The Blind Side" is set in Memphis, Tennessee, and many of the film's scenes were shot on location in the city and its surrounding areas.

Fun Fact: The film earned Sandra Bullock her first Oscar.

THE FIRM (1993)

"The Firm" is a thrilling legal drama based on John Grisham's novel. It follows attorney Mitch McDeere as he navigates a prestigious law firm in Memphis, Tennessee, that is filled with secrets and corruption. The features a stellar cast, led by Tom Cruise and Gene Hackman.

Fun Fact: "The Firm" showcases several iconic landmarks in Memphis, Tennessee, including the Peabody Hotel, Beale Street, and the Mississippi River.

THE GREEN MILE (1999)

"The Green Mile" is a compelling film set in a Louisiana prison during the 1930s. Based on Stephen King's novel of the same name, it follows the lives of guards and inmates at the prison, with a particular focus on a gentle giant named John Coffey, a death row inmate with miraculous healing powers. Through themes of compassion and redemption, the film explores profound moral dilemmas.

Fun Fact: While "The Green Mile" is primarily set in Louisiana, parts of the film were shot on location in Tennessee. The Cold Mountain Penitentiary, where much of the story takes place, was constructed on a soundstage at the Tennessee State Penitentiary in Nashville.

HANNAH MONTANA: THE MOVIE (2009)

A heartwarming comedy-drama based on the popular Disney Channel television series that follows teenager Miley Stewart as she juggles her life as pop star Hannah Montana. While "Hannah Montana: The Movie" is set in the fictional town of Crowley Corners, Tennessee, parts of the film were shot on location in Franklin and Columbia, Tennessee.

Fun Fact: This is the only theatrically-released film based on a Disney Channel original series. Also, the film features appearances by famous music stars like Taylor Swift and Rascal Flatts.

THE LAST CASTLE (2001)

A gripping drama set in a military prison, focusing on the conflict between General Eugene Irwin and Colonel Winter. The film features powerful performances from Robert Redford and James Gandolfini.

Fun Fact: Many of the scenes were filmed at the former Tennessee State Prison in Tennessee which operated from 1898 to 1992. Many significant set modifications were made to both the inside and outside including steel walkways and the guard towers.

THE MATRIX (1999)
The groundbreaking science fiction film featuring Keanu Reeves and Carrie Ann Moss, that follows the story of Neo, a computer programmer who discovers the truth about reality—that humanity is enslaved by intelligent machines, and that the world as he knows it is a simulated reality known as the Matrix.

Fun Fact: The link to Tennessee in this film might be missed if you blink. But in the opening scene where Trinity is being chased along rooftops, the skyline is clearly Nashville. What gives it away is the AT&T building, known to locals as the Batman building.

OCTOBER SKY (1999)
Based on the true story of Homer Hickam, a coal miner's son who becomes a NASA engineer, this inspiring film includes scenes shot in East Tennessee, showcasing its Appalachian landscape.

Fun Fact: The author originally wanted the film to be titled "Rocket Boys," mirroring the book it's adapted from, but the studio had concerns about its marketability. As a compromise, the title "October Sky" was chosen, which holds dual significance: it represents the month when the protagonist is initially inspired by the sight of Sputnik, and it cleverly rearranges into an anagram of "Rocket Boys."

WALK THE LINE (2005)

This Johnny Cash biopic starring Joaquin Phoenix and Reese Witherspoon follows the life of legendary musician Johnny Cash, tracing his journey from his impoverished upbringing in Arkansas to his rise to fame as one of the most influential figures in country music history.

The film was shot partly in Memphis, as well as at the Tennessee State Penitentiary in Nashville, which stood in for California's Folsom Prison in key scenes, adding authenticity to the iconic prison concert moments.

Fun Fact: Phoenix and Witherspoon performed all the singing in the film themselves, and also learned how to play their instruments (guitar and auto-harp) for the film.

18

TV SHOWS FILMED IN TENNESSEE

CHRISTY (1994–1995)
Based on the novel "Christy" by Catherine Marshall, this show follows the story of Christy Huddleston, a young woman who leaves her privileged life to become a schoolteacher in the Appalachian Mountains of Tennessee in the early 20th century. It was filmed in and around Townsend, Tennessee, near Gatlinburg.

Fun Fact: ChristyFest, a festival for all things Christy, is held every year in Townsend, Tennessee.

GEORGE & TAMMY (2022–2023)
A biographical series depicting the passionate yet tumultuous relationship between country music icons George Jones and Tammy Wynette, featuring Michael Shannon and Jessica Chastain. Set in Nashville, Tennessee, the show highlights their romantic entanglements and professional collaborations.

Fun Fact: Michael Shannon and Jessica Chastain showcase

their vocal talents by actually singing as George Jones and Tammy Wynette in the series, rather than lip-syncing.

HEE HAW (1969–1993)

A country-themed variety show that combined comedy sketches, musical performances and recurring characters. Set in the fictional community of Kornfield Kounty, the show featured beloved segments like "Pickin' and Grinnin'," and welcomed legendary guest stars from the world of country music. It was filmed in Nashville, Tennessee.

Fun Fact: With over 20 seasons and more than 600 episodes, "Hee Haw" holds the record as one of the longest-running syndicated shows in television history.

NASHVILLE (2012–2018)

A musical drama series set against the backdrop of the Nashville music scene following one star at her peak and another on the rise. Several of the actors performed their own singing in the series. The show was primarily filmed on location in Nashville.

Fun Fact: Except for the pilot, each episode of season one is named after a Hank Williams song.

STILL THE KING (2016–2017)

This comedy series featured Billy Ray Cyrus as a washed-up, one-hit-wonder who becomes an Elvis impersonator. The show was filmed in and around Nashville, Tennessee.

Fun Fact: The show's cast includes notable actors and musicians, including Joey Lauren Adams, Madison Iseman and Leslie David Baker.

SUN RECORDS (2017)

This historical drama series tells the story of the early days of rock 'n' roll and the rise of iconic musicians at Sun Records in Memphis, Tennessee. "Sun Records" was filmed on location in Memphis, Tennessee, including at the actual Sun Studio, where many of the pivotal scenes take place.

Fun Fact: The show features a talented ensemble cast portraying real-life music legends, including Elvis Presley, Johnny Cash, Jerry Lee Lewis and Carl Perkins, as well as Sun Records' founder Sam Phillips. The actors underwent extensive research and preparation to capture the essence of these iconic figures.

19
FAMOUS TENNESSEANS

Famous Actors/Actresses

ANNIE POTTS
She was born in Nashville, Tennessee, but grew up in Kentucky. Potts is best known for her role as Janine Melnitz in the "Ghostbusters" film series and as Mary Jo Shively in the CBS sitcom "Designing Women." Potts was nominated for a Primetime Emmy Award for her role in "Love & War." She has also voiced Bo Peep in the "Toy Story" films.

GINNIFER GOODWIN
Born in Memphis, Tennessee, Goodwin is best known for her roles as Snow White in the fantasy TV series "Once Upon a Time," Margene Heffman in "Big Love," and for voicing Judy Hopps in Disney's animated movie "Zootopia." Goodwin has appeared in several TV shows and movies, including "Mona Lisa Smile," "Walk the Line," "He's Just Not That Into You," and "Killing Kennedy." She changed her name from Jennifer to

Ginnifer to help it stand out and to ensure that it is pronounced correctly in accordance with her regional accent.

KATHY BATES
This Academy Award-winning actress was born in Memphis. She's perhaps most famous for her roles in "Misery," "Fried Green Tomatoes," and "Blind Side," but has had an extensive career in film and television. Bates battled ovarian and breast cancer, and she's been very open about her experiences to raise awareness.

MEGAN FOX
Born in Oakwood, Tennessee, and raised in Rockwood, Tennessee, Fox is best known for her roles in action-packed films like "Teenage Mutant Ninja Turtles" and "Transformers."

MORGAN FREEMAN
Born in Memphis, Tennessee, but raised in Mississippi, Freeman is a well-known American actor, filmmaker, and narrator famous for his distinctive, deep voice. His career spans over five decades, covering multiple film genres. Some of his best-known roles occurred in movies like "The Shawshank Redemption," "Million Dollar Baby," "Driving Miss Daisy and "Invictus." After high school, Freeman enlisted in the United States Air Force and served as a radar technician before moving to Los Angeles, California, to pursue a career in acting.

REESE WITHERSPOON
Witherspoon, an actress, producer and brilliant businesswoman, was born in New Orleans and raised in Nashville, Tennessee. She began her career in acting as a child and achieved fame with roles in "The Man in the Moon,"

"Election," "Cruel Intentions," "Wild" and as Elle Woods in "Legally Blonde." Witherspoon won an Academy Award for Best Actress for her role in "Walk the Line." Her Tennessee upbringing has significantly influenced her work and personal identity, often reflected in her film choices and public persona. She even named her youngest son, "Tennessee James."

CYNTHIA RHODES

Born in Nashville, Rhodes is known for her roles in "Dirty Dancing," "Flashdance," and "Staying Alive." She retired from acting to raise her children with her former husband, singer Richard Marx.

SAMUEL L. JACKSON

Born in Washington, D.C., Jackson grew up in Chattanooga, Tennessee. This well-known actor has appeared in over 150 films. He's best known for his roles in "Pulp Fiction" (1994), the "Jurassic Park" series, the "Star Wars" prequels and the Marvel Cinematic Universe. Before acting, Jackson intended to become a marine biologist. He was deeply impacted by the Civil Rights Movement and was an usher at Martin Luther King Jr.'s funeral.

Famous Musicians

ELVIS PRESLEY

Born in Tupelo, Mississippi, on January 8, 1935, Elvis Presley moved to Memphis, Tennessee, when he was 13 years old. It was in Memphis that his music career took off, and he became one of the most influential and iconic figures in music history.

Known as the "King of Rock and Roll," Elvis revolutionized popular music with his unique voice, electrifying performances, and the blending of gospel, blues, country, and rhythm and blues styles. His timeless hits, including "Heartbreak Hotel," "Jailhouse Rock," and "Hound Dog," continue to resonate with fans across generations.

Memphis played a crucial role in Elvis's rise to fame. Sun Studio, known as the birthplace of rock and roll, is where Elvis recorded his first song, "That's All Right," in 1954. This recording is considered one of the defining moments in the creation of rock and roll.

Memphis also became his lifelong home, where he eventually purchased Graceland, the iconic mansion that continues to draw hundreds of thousands of visitors annually. In fact, Graceland is the second-most-visited house in the U.S. after the White House.

Beyond his music, Elvis was a prolific actor, starring in over 30 feature films, including *Jailhouse Rock*, *Viva Las Vegas*, and *Blue Hawaii*. His charm and charisma translated effortlessly onto the big screen, cementing him as a pop culture icon.

Although Elvis's global fame made him a household name, he never forgot his roots. He frequently performed benefit concerts for local charities in Memphis and supported causes in his hometown.

ARETHA FRANKLIN

Franklin, often referred to as the "Queen of Soul," was born in Memphis, Tennessee. She was one of the most iconic figures in American music history. Franklin's powerful vocals and emotive delivery earned her numerous accolades, including 18 Grammy Awards. Hits like "Respect," "I Say a Little Prayer" and "(You Make Me Feel Like) A Natural Woman" are just a few examples of her timeless classics that continue to resonate with audiences worldwide.

In 2009, NASA named asteroid 25196 after the "Queen of Soul," a celestial tribute to her enduring legacy.

DOLLY PARTON

The fourth of 12 children, Parton was born in a one-room cabin in Pittman Center, Tennessee. She is a renowned American singer-songwriter, actress, brilliant businesswoman and philanthropist, known for her significant contributions to country music. She made her album debut in 1967 with "Hello, I'm Dolly," which kickstarted a successful career in the music industry. Parton has composed over 3,000 songs, including hits like "Jolene," "9 to 5," and "I Will Always Love You," which also became an international hit for Whitney Houston.

Parton's life and work extend beyond her music career. She is also known for her acting roles in films such as "9 to 5" and "Steel Magnolias," and for founding the popular Dollywood theme park in Tennessee. Her philanthropic efforts and business ventures, coupled with her musical talents, have made her not only a celebrated Tennessean but also a beloved figure worldwide.

Parton founded the Imagination Library in 1995, a program

that mails free books to children from birth until they start school, regardless of the family's income. Another fun fact about Parton is her secret song. She recorded a special song—locked away in a time capsule at her Dollywood DreamMore Resort—that cannot be heard until 2045.

MILEY CYRUS

Cyrus was born in Franklin, Tennessee, and is a multifaceted artist known for her acting and singing career. She's known for pop hits like "Party in the USA," "Wrecking Ball," and "The Climb," in addition to her recent Grammy-winning song "Flowers." She first gained fame as the lead actor in the Disney series "Hannah Montana," which launched her into stardom and paved the way for her successful music career.

Cyrus was born Destiny Hope Cyrus and was given the nickname "Smiley," which eventually evolved into "Miley," due to her cheerful disposition as a child. She legally changed her name to Miley Ray Cyrus in 2008. She is the daughter of country singer Billy Ray Cyrus, and Dolly Parton is her godmother.

KINGS OF LEON

This rock band is made up of brothers Caleb, Nathan, and Jared Followill, along with their cousin Matthew Followill. The band was formed in Nashville, Tennessee in 1999. Raised in a deeply religious household, the Followill brothers spent much of their childhood traveling throughout the southern U.S. with their father, Ivan Leon Followill, a Pentecostal preacher. When their father stepped down from preaching in 1997, Caleb and Nathan moved to Nashville and began to explore music more seriously.

The band's name, Kings of Leon, is a tribute to their grandfather Leon, who was a significant figure in their lives. They are best known for hits like "Sex on Fire" and "Use Somebody", which helped them gain international fame.

JUSTIN TIMBERLAKE
Timberlake, who hails from Memphis, Tennessee, is a Grammy Award-winning singer, songwriter, actor and record producer. He rose to fame as a member of the boy band NSYNC in the late 1990s, before establishing a successful solo career. Timberlake is known for his hit songs "SexyBack," "Cry Me a River" and "Can't Stop the Feeling!"

Timberlake frequently expresses pride in his Tennessee roots. He's called Memphis "a place you're proud to be from," and both his official fan club and his touring band are called "The Tennessee Kids."

ROY ACUFF
Known as the "King of Country Music," Roy Acuff was born in Maynardville, Tennessee. His path to music began unexpectedly after his baseball career was cut short in 1929. During tryouts with a professional team, he suffered repeated sunstrokes, which left him unable to continue pursuing the sport.

While recovering, Acuff took up the fiddle, and by 1934 he was performing on Knoxville radio. His band, first known as the "Crazy Tennesseans" and later the "Smoky Mountain Boys," marked the start of his rise in country music"

Acuff was one of the most influential figures in country music history. He was the first living artist inducted into the Country Music Hall of Fame in 1962.

TINA TURNER
Born Anna Mae Bullock in Nutbush, Tennessee, Turner was a legendary singer, songwriter and actress who was a major force in the music industry with hits like "Proud Mary" and "What's Love Got to Do with It."

Turner became a Swiss citizen in 2013, residing in Zurich, Switzerland, where she found peace and privacy away from the spotlight.

TAYLOR SWIFT
Before she became the worldwide phenomenon she is today, Swift lived in Tennessee for a time. She was born in Pennsylvania, but Swift moved to Tennessee at the age of 14, to attend high school and make it easier to break into the music scene.

She has donated a few key belongings to Nashville's Country Music Hall of Fame and Museum, including her famous glitter guitar.

Taylor Swift has given back countless times and in a variety of ways. She has donated millions to different Tennessee charities and organizations. In both 2020 and 2023 she donated a million dollars to help citizens affected by tornadoes in Tennessee. Swift has given money to the school she attended, Nashville Henderson High School, to help refurbish the auditorium. She has also given money to the Country Music Hall of Fame and Museum in Nashville to build a new education center, provided funds to the Nashville Symphony and partnered with the Tennessee Police to help protect children from predators.

Most recently, she partnered with Feeding America, donating $5 million toward hurricane relief efforts following the impacts of Hurricanes Helene and Milton.

Famous Authors

AMY GREENE
Born and raised in the foothills of East Tennessee's Smoky Mountains, Greene is best known for her New York Times bestselling debut novel "Bloodroot." Much of her writing is inspired by the stories of her family and the folklore of the region.

CATHERINE MARSHALL
Known for her fiction, non-fiction and inspirational works—including "Christy" and "A Man Called Peter,"—Marshall was born in Johnson City, Tennessee. She achieved significant success as a writer, with her books selling over 16 million copies. "Christy" was made into a television series, and her biography about her minister husband, "A Man Called Peter," was adapted into a film.

JAMES AGEE
Born in Knoxville, Tennessee, Agee was a novelist, journalist, poet, screenwriter and film critic. His most notable work was "A Death in the Family," a largely autobiographical story which won the Pulitzer Prize for fiction posthumously. Agee

also wrote the screenplay for "The African Queen" and "The Night of the Hunter."

NIKKI GIOVANNI
Born in Knoxville, Giovanni is one of America's foremost poets, and one of the world's most popular African-American poets. She's best known for her poetry collections, including "Black Feeling, Black Talk/Black Judgement." Giovanni has won many awards, been nominated for a Grammy for her poetry album, holds 27 honorary degrees and has been given the keys to multiple cities, including Dallas, New York City and Los Angeles. Nikki is a nickname given to her by her sister. Her full name is Yolande Cornelia Giovanni Jr.

ROBERT PENN WARREN
Born in Guthrie, Kentucky, but raised in Clarksville, Tennessee, Warren was a poet, critic and novelist, best known for his novel "All the King's Men," which won the Pulitzer Prize. He is the only person to have won Pulitzer Prizes for both fiction and poetry.

Other Famous Tennesseans

SEQUOYAH: CREATOR OF THE CHEROKEE SYLLABARY
Sequoyah, a remarkable figure in Native American history from Tuskegee, Tennessee, profoundly transformed Cherokee communication with the invention of the Cherokee syllabary in the early 19th century. A syllabary is a writing system that uses symbols to represent syllables, which make up words.

With no formal education, and unable to read or write in any language, Sequoyah was nonetheless fascinated by the written communication of English settlers. This fascination spurred him to dedicate years to the development of a writing system for the Cherokee language, culminating in the creation of a syllabary consisting of 86 characters, each representing a unique sound of the Cherokee language. This monumental achievement swiftly elevated the Cherokee people to an incredibly high literacy rate, surpassing that of the surrounding European-American settlers.

Sequoyah's invention played a crucial role in preserving Cherokee language and culture, marking him as one of the only individuals in history to single-handedly create an entirely new system of writing. His legacy significantly impacted Tennessee history by enriching the cultural heritage of the state and demonstrating the resilience and innovation of the Cherokee people. Through his syllabary, Sequoyah facilitated the first Native American newspaper, the Cherokee Phoenix, published in both English and Cherokee.

RHEA SEDDON
Margaret Rhea Seddon, a trailblazer from Murfreesboro, Tennessee, made history as one of NASA's first female astronauts and Tennessee's first woman in space. Initially dreaming of space while pursuing a medical career, Seddon's ambitions took flight when NASA selected her in 1978. With a medical degree from the University of Tennessee and a completed surgery residency, she spent over 700 hours in space across three missions in 1985, 1991 and 1993. Beyond her space explorations, Seddon played a crucial role as the onboard crew medical officer, researching human adaptation to space. Post-NASA, she continued her medical career at Vanderbilt

University and authored "Go for Orbit," sharing her extraordinary experiences.

She married Robert Lee "Hoot" Gibson, a fellow astronaut, and they have four children together. Their first child was humorously dubbed "The World's First Astrotot."

PAT SUMMITT

Summitt was born in Clarksville, Tennessee, and was a legendary women's basketball coach who spent her entire career at the University of Tennessee. With an impressive eight national championships under her belt, she holds the record for the highest win percentage of any Division I basketball coach, with 1,098 wins under her belt. She coached the U.S. Women's Basketball team at the 1984 Olympics and won gold.

She was asked to coach the University of Tennessee Men's basketball team on two separate occasions. She declined both offers. Her reasoning was rooted in her deep commitment to women's basketball and her belief that coaching men's basketball should not be seen as a "step up." Summitt felt strongly that women's athletics, particularly basketball, deserved the same recognition, support, and commitment as men's sports.

WILMA RUDOLPH

Wilma Rudolph, born in Saint Bethlehem, Tennessee, was an Olympic track and field athlete. She overcame childhood polio to be named the fastest woman in the world in the 1960s. During the 1960 Summer Olympics, Rudolph became the first American woman to win three gold medals in a single Olympic Games. Her remarkable achievements earned her several nicknames, including: "The Tornado," "The Black Gazelle," "The Flash," "The Black Pearl" and "Skeeter."

CORDELL HULL

Hailing from the picturesque town of Olympus, Tennessee, Hull etched his name in history as the longest-serving Secretary of State in U.S. history, spanning the crucial period of 1933 to 1944 under President Franklin D. Roosevelt. Renowned for his pivotal role in establishing the United Nations, Hull was instrumental in crafting international policies that laid the groundwork for post-World War II diplomacy. He received the Nobel Peace Prize in 1945 for his role in establishing the United Nations.

DAVY CROCKETT

Davy Crockett, the legendary American frontiersman and folk hero, left an indelible mark on Tennessee's history and mythology. Born in 1786, in what is now Greene County, Tennessee, Crockett became synonymous with the pioneer spirit of the American frontier. Known for his sharpshooting skills, Crockett was also a charismatic storyteller whose larger-than-life exploits became the stuff of legend. He served as a Tennessee state legislator and later as a member of the U.S. House of Representatives, where he championed the rights of settlers and opposed President Andrew Jackson's Indian Removal Act.

His fierce independence and colorful personality made him a folk hero in Tennessee and beyond, inspiring countless tales, songs and eventually television and film adaptations. Crockett's final stand at the Battle of the Alamo in 1836 further cemented his legacy as a symbol of bravery and freedom, and he remains a beloved figure in Tennessee's history.

JACK DANIEL

The man behind the famous whiskey, Jack Daniel, was born in Lynchburg, Tennessee, and began his entrepreneurial journey young. At just 10 years old, he apprenticed under Nathan "Nearest" Green, an enslaved man and skilled distiller who taught him the unique charcoal mellowing process that would become the hallmark of Jack Daniel's Tennessee whiskey. This technique, now known as the Lincoln County Process, gives the whiskey its distinctive smooth flavor.

NEAREST GREEN

Though he may not be a household name, Nathan "Nearest" Green deserves recognition as the first known Black master distiller in the U.S. An enslaved man, Green taught Jack Daniel the art of whiskey distillation in Lynchburg, Tennessee, in the mid-1800s.

Known as "Uncle Nearest," Green's expertize in the unique charcoal mellowing process—now a hallmark of Tennessee whiskey—set Jack Daniel's whiskey apart, establishing the smooth flavor that made it famous. After the Civil War, Daniel hired Green as his distillery's first master distiller, a groundbreaking role that should have brought Green widespread fame.

Thanks to Fawn Weaver, a researcher and whiskey entrepreneur, Green's legacy now lives on through the Uncle Nearest Premium Whiskey brand, honoring his contributions to Tennessee's whiskey heritage and bringing his remarkable story to light.

SAMUEL POWHATON CARTER

Samuel Powhatan Carter stands alone in American history as the only person to ever serve as both an Admiral in the Navy and a General in the Army. Born into the rolling hills of Elizabethton, Tennessee, Carter's extraordinary military career spanned both land and sea, showcasing an unparalleled versatility and dedication to his country.

ANDREW JACKSON

Originally from the Carolinas, Jackson lived much of his life in Tennessee. He was the 7th U.S. President and served as a U.S. Senator representing Tennessee. Jackson's plantation home in Tennessee, the Hermitage, was one of the first homes in the United States to have indoor plumbing, including a flush toilet that they named "The Ajax." He was the only president to have been a prisoner of war, having been captured by the British during the American Revolutionary War. Known for his fiery personality, he taught his African Grey parrot to curse and it had to be removed from his funeral for swearing.

SUPERSTITIONS, MYTHS & MYSTERIOUS CREATURES

THE BELL WITCH
The Bell Witch legend is one of Tennessee's most haunting tales, originating in the early 19th century on the Bell family farm in Adams, Robertson County. This unsettling story centers on a malevolent entity that tormented the Bell family, particularly targeting the father, John Bell, and his youngest daughter, Betsy. What began as strange noises escalated to physical attacks, eventually leading to John Bell's mysterious death. Many believe he was poisoned, with some attributing his demise to the vengeful actions of the Bell Witch.

THE TALE OF THE BELL WITCH'S KINDNESS
While the Bell Witch is predominantly known for her malevolence, there's a lesser-known side to the legend that speaks of her protecting the Bell family from harm. In some versions of the story, the entity displayed moments of care, especially towards Lucy Bell, John Bell's wife, offering comfort and even singing hymns to her. This complexity adds depth to the

legend, suggesting that not all interactions were rooted in terror.

THE BELL WITCH CAVE

Bell Witch Cave. Photo by Www78, CC BY-SA 3.0, via Wikimedia Commons

The Bell Witch Cave, a key landmark tied to the legend, is said to be the witch's dwelling and plays a crucial role in the story's endurance. Visitors are drawn to this cave, seeking connections to the eerie events that unfolded over 200 years ago.

THE LEGEND OF JOHN MURRELL'S THUMB

John Murrell, a notorious bandit and land pirate who operated along the Mississippi River in the early 19th century, is said to have buried his treasures in various locations throughout Tennessee. According to legend, Murrell's thumb, cut off after his death to prevent him from returning as a malevolent spirit, was also buried separately to confuse and guard the locations of his hidden loot.

THE ETERNAL FLAME FALLS IN CHATTANOOGA

Nestled in the Chattanooga region, there's a natural gas leak that keeps a small flame burning behind a waterfall, known as the Eternal Flame Falls. The Cherokee have a romantic legend that the flame was lit by a lover's broken heart, promising eternal love. This natural wonder, combined with the legend, creates a magical and romantic setting.

THE LEGEND OF OLD GREEN EYES

This story hails from the Chickamauga Battlefield in Chattanooga, the site of one of the Civil War's bloodiest battles. Old Green Eyes is said to be a spirit—either a fallen soldier with glowing green eyes or a creature pre-dating the Civil War—that roams the battlefield. Despite its potentially eerie origins, many see Old Green Eyes as a guardian of the fallen, adding a layer of mystique and protection over the sacred ground.

THE WOODBOOGER OF BIG RIDGE STATE PARK

The Woodbooger is a creature said to inhabit the dense forests of Big Ridge State Park and other wooded areas of Tennessee. The term "Woodbooger" is sometimes used in Appalachian regions to describe a Bigfoot-like creature, suggesting a large, hairy being that lives in the woods, away from human settlements. Reports often describe it as shy, elusive and more curious than threatening.

THE TENNESSEE WILDMAN

Descriptions portray the Wildman as a large, hairy humanoid with incredible speed and strength, known for its frightening scream and occasionally aggressive behavior towards humans. Unlike the Woodbooger, which is usually associated with specific wooded areas and might be part of broader Bigfoot folklore, the Tennessee Wildman is often described as a strange creature with a distinct backstory. According to some tales, the Wildman was a circus escapee who took to the woods, while others suggest it's a native creature of the Tennessee wilderness.

21
FAMOUS ATTRACTIONS & UNIQUE FESTIVALS

Famous Attractions

GREAT SMOKY MOUNTAINS NATIONAL PARK

Great Smoky Mountains National Park. Photo by dndavis via depostphotos.com

The Great Smoky Mountains National Park is not just a natural wonder, it's a premier destination for millions of tourists each year, offering a variety of attractions and activities. The park is home to a collection of celebrated log buildings, and over 90 other historic structures maintained in their original settings, including barns, churches, schools and mills.

With an average of over 12 million visitors a year, the Great Smoky Mountain National Park is the most visited national park in the United States, by a long shot. The Grand Canyon comes in second with around 4.7 million visitors a year. Zion National Park is right behind with an average of 4.6 million visitors each year.

Great Smoky Mountains National Park is unique as it does not charge an entrance fee. This policy is rooted in the historical legal actions and agreements made when the park was established. In 1951, the state of Tennessee transferred two important roads to the park with the restriction that no tolls could be charged on these roads. A federal law (16 U.S. Code) later reinforced this by preventing the National Park Service from charging entrance fees where tolls are prohibited on primary park roads.

While there is no entrance fee, the park does charge for camping and parking to help fund maintenance and services.

SYNCHRONOUS FIREFLIES OF GREAT SMOKY MOUNTAINS

Each year, the park hosts a natural light show by the synchronous fireflies, which are unique for their ability to synchronize their flashing patterns. This phenomenon draws visitors from around the world and is one of the park's most magical attractions.

The best time to see this spectacular event is in late May to early June. The peak display lasts for about two weeks each year, but the exact timing can vary depending on temperature and soil moisture. The most popular viewing spot is the Elkmont area of the park.

Due to the high demand, the National Park Service uses a lottery system to manage parking and ensure a safe and enjoyable experience for all visitors. The lottery to apply for a vehicle pass opens for a few days in April each year. Successful applicants are notified in mid-May, and the viewing period usually spans from early to mid-June. All details can be found at recreation.gov.

GRACELAND

Graceland. Photo by Victor Hamberlin via Flickr.

Graceland is the home of Elvis Presley, the King of Rock 'n' Roll, and is one of the most visited private homes in the U.S. In fact, with over 650,000 visitors a year, it is the second most-visited house in the U.S. after the White House. The name "Graceland" was chosen by the original owners, Thomas and Ruth Moore, and is named after Ruth's aunt, Grace Toof. Elvis Presley purchased Graceland at the age of 22 in 1957 for $105,000, which equals about $1,159,581 in 2024. Today, the mansion and its grounds are worth an estimated $100 million.

The mansion, built in 1939 in the Colonial Revival style, has 23 rooms, including eight bedrooms and eight bathrooms. There's a "secret" room upstairs that has remained untouched since the day Elvis passed away. Only a few people have ever been allowed upstairs, to maintain the privacy and respect for the Presley family. Graceland receives so much mail from fans around the world that it has its own zip code: 38116.

The Meditation Garden, where Elvis and his family are buried, is located on the grounds of Graceland.

DOLLYWOOD
Dollywood, nestled in the scenic Smoky Mountains of Pigeon Forge, Tennessee, is a beloved theme park co-owned by country music legend Dolly Parton and Herschend Family Entertainment. Dolly Parton became involved in 1986 when the park was renamed from Silver Dollar City to Dollywood.

More than just a destination for thrilling rides and entertainment, Dollywood is a celebration of the rich Appalachian culture that Parton herself grew up in. The park features traditional crafts, music and performances that pay homage to the region's heritage.

A visit to Dollywood is not complete without trying the famous cinnamon bread, freshly baked at the Grist Mill. This delicious treat has become a must-have for visitors, with some even claiming it's the highlight of their trip.

Dollywood has a Calming Room designed for sensory-sensitive guests who might need a quiet, relaxing environment during their visit. This calming room was one of the first of its kind at any theme park in the world.

Dollywood is home to the American Eagle Foundation's Eagle Mountain Sanctuary, hosting the country's largest presentation of non-releasable bald eagles. The sanctuary allows visitors to observe these majestic birds up close, contributing to wildlife conservation efforts.

Tucked away in the park is Dolly Parton's own secret apartment, a cozy and beautifully decorated space where she stays during her visits. Though off-limits to the public, it's said to reflect Parton's style and warmth.

THE SECRET CITY
Oak Ridge, known as the "Secret City," was established in 1942 by the U.S. government as part of the top-secret Manhattan Project during World War II, aimed at developing the atomic bomb.

Initially planned to house 13,000 people, Oak Ridge's population soared to 75,000 by the end of the war, making it the fifth-largest city in Tennessee at the time. The city was constructed at a record pace, with homes, schools and facilities springing up almost overnight.

Billboard posted in Oak Ridge, Tennessee, 1943. Photo by Ed Westcott / United States Department of Energy, Public Domain

Despite its secretive nature, Oak Ridge functioned as a typical American town in many ways. It had stores, schools, movie theaters and even its own symphony orchestra led by a Manhattan Project scientist.

After World War II, Oak Ridge transitioned from a secretive wartime project to a hub for scientific research and development. The Oak Ridge National Laboratory continues to be a leader in various fields, including nuclear medicine and space exploration. The city also played a role in the early space program by providing materials and testing for NASA.

Today, visitors can explore Oak Ridge's rich history at the Manhattan Project National Historical Park, which includes sites like the American Museum of Science and Energy, the X-

10 Graphite Reactor, and various historical neighborhoods and buildings that tell the story of this unique city and its impact on the world.

NATIONAL CIVIL RIGHTS MUSEUM

Lorraine Motel, Memphis, TN. Photo by Bubba73, CC BY-SA 3.0, via Wikimedia Commons

Tennessee's National Civil Rights Museum isn't your typical museum. Housed within the Lorraine Motel—the very spot where Dr. Martin Luther King, Jr. was assassinated on April 4 — 1968, the museum offers a powerful and moving experience.

The motel, once an upscale lodging for Black clientele during segregation, has hosted many notable musicians, including Otis Redding, Aretha Franklin and Ray Charles.

After King's assassination, the motel fell into decline and faced foreclosure. Efforts by local business leaders and the newly established Martin Luther King Memphis Memorial Foundation saved the property. The foundation purchased the motel in 1982 and eventually secured funds from the state, county and city to develop it into a museum, which officially opened in 1991.

The museum features over 260 artifacts, more than 40 films, oral histories and interactive media. Notable exhibits include Room 306, preserved as it was when King was assassinated, and the Legacy Building, which explores the investigation into King's assassination. Other powerful exhibits highlight key events such as the Montgomery Bus Boycott and the Freedom Rides.

THE LOST SEA ADVENTURE
The Lost Sea Adventure, located in Sweetwater, Tennessee, offers an extraordinary journey into America's largest underground lake, the Lost Sea. Part of the extensive Craighead Caverns, this vast body of water lies 140 feet (42.6 meters) below ground level and spans over 4.5 acres (1.8 hectare).

While many visitors are drawn to the clear, tranquil waters, few know that the caverns have a rich history dating back thousands of years. The cave was used by Native Americans, as evidenced by the discovery of ancient artifacts such as pottery and weapons.

During the Civil War, Confederate soldiers mined the cave for saltpeter, a key component in gunpowder production. The lake itself is home to a population of rainbow trout, originally introduced in the 1960s to control algae growth. Despite the absence of natural light, these fish have thrived, adding to the unique charm of this subterranean wonder.

THE BATMAN BUILDING AKA THE AT&T BUILDING

AT&T Building in Nashville. Photo by Donnie King

The AT&T building in downtown Nashville is nicknamed The Batman Building because its distinctive silhouette resembles the caped crusader's mask. It also happens to be the tallest building in Tennessee, and its twin spires are a prominent feature of the Nashville skyline.

SUNSPHERE IN KNOXVILLE

Sunsphere in Knoxville. Photo by sepavone via depositphotos.com

This iconic structure in Knoxville was built for the 1982 World's Fair and stands 266 feet (81 meters) tall. The Sunsphere offers an observation deck with a 360-degree view of the city and the Great Smoky Mountains. Its golden glass panels and distinctive design make it a must-see landmark in Tennessee.

THE CONCRETE PARTHENON IN NASHVILLE

Parthenon in Tennessee. Photo by zrfphoto via depositphoto.com

A full-scale replica of the original Parthenon in Athens stands in Nashville as a monument to what is considered the pinnacle of classical architecture. Inside, it houses a 42-foot (12.8 meters) statue of Athena, considered the largest indoor sculpture in the Western world.

THE RYMAN AUDITORIUM

The Ryman Auditorium in Nashville, Tennessee, is one of the most iconic and historically significant music venues in the United States, famously known as the "Mother Church of Country Music."

The Ryman Auditorium. Photo by Daniel Schwen, CC BY-SA 4.0, via Wikimedia Commons

Built in 1892 as the Union Gospel Tabernacle by Captain Tom Ryman, it was renamed in his honor after his death in 1904. From 1943 to 1974, it served as the home of the Grand Ole Opry, greatly enhancing its fame. Although the Ryman fell into disrepair after the Opry moved in 1974, a major restoration in the 1990s revitalized the venue.

The Ryman Auditorium is renowned for its outstanding acoustics, which are considered some of the best in the world.

DID YOU KNOW?

The Ryman is said to be haunted by several ghosts, including country music legend Hank Williams Sr., and that of Captain Tom Ryman himself.

THE GRAND OLE OPRY IN NASHVILLE

Grand Ole Opry. Photo by Glen E via Flickr

The Grand Ole Opry, a weekly country music stage concert, is the longest-running radio broadcast in U.S. history, starting in 1925. Originating as the "WSM Barn Dance," it was renamed by George D. Hay in 1927.

Held at the Ryman Auditorium from 1943 to 1974, the Opry then moved to the Grand Ole Opry House, also in Nashville, Tennessee, where it remains today. The Opry returns to the Ryman in winter, however, and a six-foot circle of oak wood from the Ryman stage is inlaid in the Opry House stage, connecting the venue's historic past with its present.

The Grand Ole Opry is performed before a live audience every week, creating an intimate and electric atmosphere that is broadcast to millions of listeners around the world. Performing at the Opry is a prestigious honor in country music. Members who have performed there include legends like Hank Williams, Patsy Cline, Garth Brooks and Carrie Underwood.

TENNESSEE'S MILLION-DOLLAR MULE CLIFF PAINTING

The Liberty Mule, a whimsical cliff painting in Liberty, Tennessee, overlooks Highway 70 in Liberty, Tennessee. This iconic silhouette of a mule, known locally as "Maud," has been a cherished local landmark for over a century.

The true origins of the mule painting were shrouded in mystery until it was discovered that Dr. Wayne Robinson, a local college student at the time, painted it in 1906. Robinson drew inspiration from the popular comic strip And Her Name Was Maud by Frederick Opper. He used coal tar to trace the mule's silhouette, intending the piece as a playful prank rather than a symbol of local culture or history.

In 2003, the community feared the mule might be lost to a multi-million-dollar highway expansion project by the Tennessee Department of Transportation, which would require blasting near the site. Residents passionately rallied with a "Save the Mule" campaign, highlighting the painting's cultural significance. Their efforts were successful; the highway department confirmed that the Liberty Mule would remain untouched, ensuring Maud's safety for future generations.

Unique Festivals

THE MULE CAPITAL OF THE WORLD

Columbia, Tennessee lays claim to the title "Mule Capital of the World." This isn't just a hollow boast! Every year, Columbia throws a massive "Mule Day" celebration. This multi-day extravaganza has been running since the 1840s. It started as a simple breeder's meet-up but now attracts over 200,000 people with mule shows, mule-driving contests, parades, contests of strength and even a Mule Day Queen!

UNICOI COUNTY APPLE FESTIVAL

For over 40 years, the Unicoi County Apple Festival has taken place in Erwin, Tennessee. This annual two-day festival celebrates the region's rich apple heritage. Every October, this cherished event attracts over 110,000 visitors and features over 350 vendors, who offer crafts and apple-themed goods. A highlight is the diverse array of apple-based foods, including pies, ciders and butters. The festival also hosts the unique "Miss Apple Festival" pageant, celebrating local beauty and talent—with an apple twist.

RC-MOON PIE FESTIVAL

Held annually in June in the charming town of Bell Buckle this festival celebrates two Southern staples: RC Cola and Moon Pies. Originating over 25 years ago, the festival features a parade, live music, dancing, games and—of course—plenty of RC Colas and Moon Pies. Bell Buckle is also known for being the smallest town in Tennessee, with a population of just over 400 people.

NATIONAL BANANA PUDDING FESTIVAL

The National Banana Pudding Festival celebrates America's favorite banana-based dessert and has been a staple in Centerville, Tennessee, for over a decade. This two-day event in October not only features a national cook-off for the best banana pudding in the country but also offers live entertainment, crafts and a "Puddin' Path," where attendees can taste multiple variations of homemade banana pudding. An interesting tidbit: the festival contributes to local nonprofits, making it a delicious way to support the community.

NATIONAL CORNBREAD FESTIVAL

The National Cornbread Festival, held annually in South Pittsburg, Tennessee, has celebrated the Southern staple of cornbread every last full weekend in April since 1996. Highlighted by the National Cornbread Cook-Off, where contestants whip up innovative cornbread recipes in Lodge Cast Iron skillets, the festival draws visitors with its lively mix of live music, arts, crafts and Southern cuisine. Notably, the event features Cornbread Alley, where attendees can sample unique cornbread dishes, and the proceeds benefit the local community.

SECRET CITY FESTIVAL

Every June in Oak Ridge, you can attend the Secret City Festival to celebrates the city's unique history as the "Secret City" during World War II, when it played a pivotal role in the Manhattan Project. The festival features a mix of music, arts, historical displays, science exhibits and family-friendly activities. It's a way for visitors and residents alike to engage with the city's rich scientific heritage and enjoy various cultural and recreational activities. The Secret City Festival typically includes WWII reenactments, tours of historical sites and other educational opportunities that highlight Oak Ridge's significant contributions to science and history.

TOMATO ART FEST

This unique and vibrant festival takes place annually in East Nashville's historic Five Points area. Celebrated since 2004, the Tomato Art Fest brings together the community through a love for tomatoes, featuring a mix of art, music, food, wacky costumes, contests and activities for all ages. The festival highlights include tomato-themed art installations, live performances and interactive exhibits, making it a fun and festive experience for residents and visitors alike.

TIN PAN SOUTH

This annual event is hosted in Nashville and is celebrated as the world's largest songwriter festival. It features hundreds of songwriters, who perform across multiple venues throughout Nashville. The festival, organized by the Nashville Songwriters Association International (NSAI), highlights songwriters across various genres, providing them with a platform to share the songs and stories behind their music. The event includes "songwriter in the round" shows, where songwriters perform and tell stories in an intimate setting, typically at Nashville's top music venues.

TENNESSEE RENAISSANCE FESTIVAL

While many U.S. states host renaissance festivals, the Tennessee Renaissance Festival stands out as the only one held on the grounds of a real castle in North America. Since 1986, every weekend in May, Castle Gwynn comes alive with medieval splendor.

Castle Gwynn, a replica of a 12th-century Welsh border castle, is the home of professional photographer Mike Freeman and his wife, Jackie. The Freemans reside in the north tower, opening the south tower to curious guests each year during the festival. This unique venue offers visitors a chance to explore the castle, and then enjoy events such as jousting tournaments, human chess games and indulging in giant turkey legs.

Each May, over 70,000 people flock to experience the magic of the Tennessee Renaissance Festival, making it a must-visit event. Interestingly, 'Gwynn' is Welsh for 'white,' adding a touch of wonder to the name—literally translating to 'white castle.'

DID YOU KNOW?

Taylor Swift brought fame to Castle Gwynn by filming parts of her 'Love Story' music video there in 2008. Originally, the plan was to shoot in a European castle to reflect the Romeo and Juliet theme (but with a happy ending) in the song. However, upon discovering the castle in Middle Tennessee, where Swift lived, the team chose it as the filming location. The rest, as they say, is history.

22
WAYS TO SEE & EXPLORE TENNESSEE

Tennessee, with its vibrant culture, rich history and stunning natural landscapes, offers a myriad of ways to experience its unique charm. From the neon-lit streets of Nashville to the majestic peaks of the Smoky Mountains, the state invites visitors to explore its musical soul, culinary delights and scenic beauty. Whether you're a history buff, sports fanatic or someone seeking haunted adventures, Tennessee has something to captivate every traveler.

Music Tours

EXPLORING NASHVILLE'S MUSIC ROW
Begin your musical journey on Nashville's Music Row, a dazzling district alive with the echoes of country legends past and present. This area, dense with recording studios and music

publishing houses, is the pulsing heart of Nashville's entertainment industry.

RCA Studio B with Historical Marker. Photo by Brent Moore via Flickr

Tour RCA Studio B, where Elvis Presley recorded over 200 songs. Music enthusiasts will revel in the rich histories recounted at the Country Music Hall of Fame and the Johnny Cash Museum. For a live music experience steeped in history, catch a show at the Ryman Auditorium or see a performance at the Grand Ole Opry, where the spirit of country music lives on every night.

THE SOULFUL STREETS OF MEMPHIS
Head west to Memphis, where Beale Street buzzes with blues at every turn. This historic street is where blues icon B.B. King made his mark, and where the sound of soul meets Southern hospitality. Visit the legendary Sun Studio, known as the birthplace of rock 'n' roll, where pioneers like Johnny Cash and Jerry Lee Lewis recorded their genre-defining tracks. No trip to

Memphis is complete without a visit to Graceland, the opulent mansion of Elvis Presley, showcasing an intimate glimpse into the life of the King of Rock 'n' Roll.

BRISTOL: THE TWIN CITY WITH A MUSICAL HEART

Travel to the northeastern tip of Tennessee to Bristol, a city that shares its heritage and main street with Virginia. Known as the "Birthplace of Country Music," Bristol was where the 1927 Bristol Sessions recordings, sometimes called the "big bang" of country music, were made. These recordings introduced the world to the Carter Family and Jimmie Rodgers. Delve into this rich history at the Birthplace of Country Music Museum, and don't miss the Bristol Rhythm & Roots Reunion—an annual celebration that features performances from hundreds of artists across multiple stages.

KNOXVILLE'S MELODIC CONTRIBUTIONS

In Knoxville, experience the vibrant "Scruffy City" music scene with a visit to the WDVX Blue Plate Special, a live performance radio show that features a mix of known and up-and-coming artists. Each March, the city hosts the Big Ears Festival, renowned for its eclectic and avant-garde performances that span genres from classical to jazz, and everything in between.

A NOD TO MUSCLE SHOALS

While just outside Tennessee, Muscle Shoals, Alabama, has a musical influence that permeates the Tennessee Valley. A short drive from the Tennessee state line takes you to this small town that boasts big history. At the Muscle Shoals Sound Studio and FAME Studios, artists like Aretha Franklin and the Rolling Stones recorded hits. A visit here offers a comprehensive understanding of the region's impact on the international music scene.

TIPS FOR MUSIC LOVERS

When planning your music tour, consider visiting during one of the many festivals for a truly immersive experience. Check venue calendars in advance to snag tickets to popular shows, and explore less touristy spots for authentic, spontaneous performances. Each city offers a unique slice of Tennessee's musical heritage.

Taste of Tennessee: Culinary Trails

SAVOR THE FLAVORS OF MEMPHIS: BBQ & BEYOND

Begin your culinary journey in Memphis, renowned for its smoky barbecue and soul food. The city's barbecue is characterized by its unique style of slow-cooked ribs, prepared "wet" (basted with sauce) or "dry" (seasoned with a dry rub). Visit iconic joints like Central BBQ and Payne's to sample these local specialties. For an authentic soul food experience, venture to The Four Way, where culinary traditions are steeped in history and community.

NASHVILLE'S HOT CHICKEN & SOUTHERN BITES

No culinary tour of Tennessee would be complete without tasting Nashville's famous hot chicken, a must-try for spice enthusiasts. Hattie B's and Prince's Hot Chicken Shack offer fiery flavors that are as much a part of the Music City's identity as country music. For a broader taste of Southern cooking, indulge in the meat-and-three offerings at Arnold's Country Kitchen, where the plates are piled high with hearty, comforting fare.

EAST TENNESSEE'S APPALACHIAN CUISINE

In East Tennessee, the culinary scene offers a deep dive into Appalachian cuisine, rooted in the natural bounty of the region. In cities like Knoxville and towns like Jonesborough, you'll find dishes that emphasize farm-to-table freshness. Restaurants like The Tomato Head in Knoxville showcase local ingredients in innovative ways. For a traditional experience, visit a local cidery or distillery to taste craft beverages that draw on age-old Appalachian traditions.

THE INTERNATIONAL FLAVORS OF CHATTANOOGA

Chattanooga is emerging as a culinary hotspot, where Southern comfort food meets international influence. Enjoy a meal at Easy Bistro & Bar, which creatively melds local flavors with French and Mediterranean techniques. For those who enjoy a global palate, Chattanooga's Public House offers dishes that blend Southern ingredients with flavors from around the world, ensuring a dining experience that's both familiar and surprising.

THE WHISKEY TRAIL: SIPPING THROUGH TENNESSEE

Tennessee's whiskey heritage offers a spirited journey through the state. Tour the Tennessee Whiskey Trail, which features over 30 distilleries. Ranging from boutique setups to world-famous brands like Jack Daniel's in Lynchburg and George Dickel in Tullahoma, visitors can learn about the traditional methods of Tennessee whiskey-making and enjoy tastings that highlight the rich, mellow flavors unique to Tennessee whiskey.

CULINARY EVENTS AND FOOD FESTIVALS

Plan your visit to coincide with one of Tennessee's many food festivals to experience the local culture and cuisine at its most festive. The National Cornbread Festival in South Pittsburg celebrates Southern cooking with a focus on cornbread, a staple of Tennessee cuisine. Memphis in May honors the culinary traditions of Memphis BBQ with a world-class barbecue cooking contest.

TIPS FOR CULINARY TRAVELERS

When embarking on a culinary tour of Tennessee, be sure to check restaurant hours and book reservations where necessary, as some popular spots can have long wait times. Consider taking a food tour or cooking class to deepen your appreciation of the local cuisine. Always ask locals for their personal recommendations to discover hidden gems.

Historical Sites

WALK THROUGH HISTORY IN MEMPHIS

Start your historical journey in Memphis, a city steeped in the rich tapestry of American music, civil rights and ancient civilizations. Visit the National Civil Rights Museum at the Lorraine Motel, where Dr. Martin Luther King Jr. was assassinated in 1968. This museum offers an immersive experience through the struggle for civil rights in America, and highlights key events that shaped the movement. Not far from here, explore the Chucalissa Archaeological Museum, a Mississippian culture site that gives insights into the lives of Native Americans in the region before European contact.

EXPLORE THE BIRTH OF COUNTRY MUSIC IN BRISTOL

Head to Bristol, recognized as the birthplace of country music from the 1927 Bristol Sessions. The Birthplace of Country Music Museum not only celebrates these recordings but also delves into the cultural impact of Appalachian music and its evolution into modern country music. This site offers a deep dive into the roots of a genre that has shaped much of American music culture.

CIVIL WAR BATTLEFIELDS

Tennessee's strategic importance during the Civil War makes it home to some of the most well-preserved battlefields in the nation. Tour the Stones River National Battlefield in Murfreesboro, which commemorates one of the bloodiest conflicts of the Civil War and played a crucial role in the Union's victory. Another significant site is the Shiloh National Military Park, which preserves the site of the early April 1862 battle, and offers interpretive programs and historical reenactments.

FORT PILLOW STATE HISTORIC PARK

Fort Pillow, located in Henning, is notable for its natural beauty and its complex history during the Civil War, including the controversial Battle of Fort Pillow, which ended in a massacre. The park now offers a museum, hiking trails, and bird-watching opportunities, and serves as a thoughtful place for learning about the darker chapters of America's past while appreciating the peace of its present nature settings.

FORT DONELSON: A TURNING POINT IN THE CIVIL WAR

Travel to Dover to explore Fort Donelson National Battlefield, where in 1862, Union forces won a significant victory early in the Civil War. This victory opened the Cumberland River as an avenue for the invasion of the South. The park offers tours, educational programs, and scenic views of the Cumberland River.

TIPS FOR HISTORY BUFFS

When visiting historical sites, consider hiring a guide or joining a tour to gain deeper insights and stories that are often not covered in self-guided tours. Check for special events or living history demonstrations that many sites offer throughout the year to see history come to life. Always check operating hours and ticketing options in advance, especially during peak tourist seasons.

Tennessee Train Adventures

Tennessee Valley Railroad Museum's diesel electric locomotive. Photo by Bob Holler via Flickr.

TENNESSEE VALLEY RAILROAD: CHATTANOOGA'S ROLLING MUSEUM

Start your rail journey with the Tennessee Valley Railroad in Chattanooga. This moving museum offers a variety of rides on restored vintage trains that provide a window into the golden age of rail travel. The most popular is the Missionary Ridge Local, a short trip that includes a turn on a turntable and a tour of the restoration shop. For a longer, more scenic experience, the Hiwassee Loop ride follows a path along the beautiful Hiwassee River through the lower Appalachian Mountains, offering breathtaking views and a relaxing ride.

THE MUSIC CITY STAR: NASHVILLE'S COMMUTER LINE WITH A VIEW

For those staying in Nashville, the Music City Star provides a fantastic way to see parts of Middle Tennessee not easily accessible by car. This commuter train runs from Nashville to Lebanon with several stops along the way. While primarily for commuters, tourists can use it on weekdays to explore the small towns and countryside of Tennessee's heartland, experiencing local life beyond the city's bustling music scene.

SECRET CITY EXCURSION TRAIN: A JOURNEY THROUGH ATOMIC HISTORY

Operated by the Southern Appalachia Railway Museum, the Secret City Scenic Excursion Train offers a trip through the Oak Ridge area, known historically as the "Secret City" for its role in the Manhattan Project during World War II. This train journey provides not only scenic views, but also a fascinating narrative about the region's critical role in atomic history. The ride is both educational and picturesque, making it a great addition to any Tennessee train adventure.

TIPS FOR TRAIN TRAVELERS

When planning your rail adventures in Tennessee:

- Check the operating days and availability of each train ride, as some are seasonal or run on limited days of the week.
- Consider themed rides, especially during holidays or special events, which often offer unique experiences like dinner trains or rides with historical reenactments.
- Book tickets in advance, especially for popular routes or special event trains which can sell out quickly.
- Prepare for the weather, as some excursions involve outdoor activities or stops where you can explore.

Tennessee Ghost Tours

THE SHADOWY STREETS OF MEMPHIS
Begin your ghostly adventures in Memphis, where history and mystery intertwine. Join a ghost tour through the historic district and discover the haunted side of iconic sites like the Orpheum Theatre, where the spirit of a young girl named Mary reportedly lingers, delighting and spooking patrons. Explore the eerie hallways of the Woodruff-Fontaine House, where ghostly encounters with the mansion's former residents are a chilling highlight. These tours provide a blend of local lore, historical facts and spine-tingling stories.

NASHVILLE'S HAUNTED PAST
In Nashville, the spirits of music legends and historical figures alike are said to roam. Take a ghost tour of the Ryman Auditorium, known as the "Mother Church of Country Music," where some say the spirits of performers like Hank Williams still take the stage. Wander through the Tennessee State Capitol, where the ghost of William Strickland, the building's architect who is entombed on the grounds, is said to still oversee his creation. Each stop on Nashville's ghost tours reveals a layer of the city's storied and spectral past.

CHATTANOOGA'S GHOSTLY ADVENTURES
Venture into Chattanooga for a ghost tour that combines the natural beauty of the mountains with the chilling tales of the city's old buildings. Visit the haunted Read House Hotel, where the spirit of Annalisa Netherly, a guest who met a grisly end in room 311, is said to cause eerie disturbances. The tours

not only scare but also enchant, as they traverse Chattanooga's downtown and the shadowy corners where history lingers in the air.

KNOXVILLE'S DARK SIDE

In Knoxville, dive deep into the city's darker corridors with a ghost tour that explores the Old City and its Victorian buildings. Hear tales of the spirits that haunt the Bijou Theatre, a former civil war hospital where it's said that not all the soldiers left! Explore the shadowy passageways beneath the city streets, where forgotten spirits are rumored to echo the footsteps of the living.

Bijou Theatre. Photo by Aaron Campbell via Flickr.

APPALACHIAN GHOST STORIES IN THE SMOKIES

For those brave enough, venture into the Great Smoky Mountains for ghost tours that explore the park's eerie history and the folklore of the Appalachian settlers. These tours often take place in the fading light of dusk, adding an extra layer of mystique. Listen to tales of lost settlers, ancient Cherokee legends, and the mysterious lights known as the "Will-o'-the-Wisps" that lead travelers astray.

ELKMONT GHOST TOWN, GREAT SMOKY MOUNTAINS NATIONAL PARK

Elkmont began as a logging town and later became a resort community before being abandoned. Now part of the Great Smoky Mountains National Park, this ghost town offers a hauntingly beautiful walk through early 20th-century vacation cottages and the remnants of the Wonderland Hotel, providing a glimpse into the past and the area's development over the years.

TIPS FOR GHOST TOUR ENTHUSIASTS

When embarking on ghost tours in Tennessee:

- Book in advance, especially around Halloween when tours can fill up quickly.
- Wear comfortable walking shoes, as many tours involve a fair amount of walking, sometimes on cobblestone streets or uneven paths.
- Bring a camera and a flashlight; you never know when you might catch an unexplained phenomenon—or simply need to illuminate your path.
- Keep an open mind and a good sense of humor. Whether you're a skeptic or a believer, ghost tours offer a fun and engaging way to learn about the history of these haunted locales.

Sporting Life: Tennessee Sports

TENNESSEE TITANS: NFL ACTION IN NASHVILLE

Dive into the heart of Tennessee's professional sports scene with a Tennessee Titans NFL game at Nissan Stadium in Nashville. The electric atmosphere on game days is something every sports fan should experience. The Titans bring thrilling football action and a passionate fan base that lights up the city on game days. Before the game, enjoy the tailgating experience with local fans, a tradition that combines food, fun, and football.

UNIVERSITY OF TENNESSEE VOLUNTEERS: COLLEGE SPORTS SPIRIT

Head to Knoxville to experience the fervor of college sports with the University of Tennessee Volunteers. Neyland Stadium, one of the largest stadiums in the country, is where the Volunteers' football team battles it out in front of over 100,000 cheering fans. The spirit of the "Vol Navy" — boats that tailgate on the Tennessee River — adds a unique touch to game days. Besides football, the Volunteers' basketball teams at Thompson-Boling Arena provide year-round excitement.

MEMPHIS GRIZZLIES: NBA EXCITEMENT

Catch the Memphis Grizzlies in action at the FedExForum in downtown Memphis for top-tier NBA basketball. The Grizzlies' games are known for their high energy and family-friendly entertainment, making it a perfect outing for sports enthusiasts of all ages. The arena is also part of the vibrant Beale Street district, allowing fans to combine a game day with some of Memphis' famous live music and dining.

NASHVILLE PREDATORS: HOCKEY AT ITS BEST

Experience the chill of NHL hockey with the Nashville Predators at Bridgestone Arena. The Predators offer fast-paced hockey action and one of the most engaging game-day experiences in the NHL, known for its loud and proud fan base and the tradition of throwing catfish onto the ice. The arena's location in downtown Nashville ensures that the energy spills over into the streets, where live music and sports celebrations blend seamlessly.

CHATTANOOGA LOOKOUTS: MINOR LEAGUE CHARM

For a more intimate sporting experience, catch a Chattanooga Lookouts baseball game at AT&T Field. This minor league team offers affordable family entertainment and the chance to see future major league stars in the early stages of their careers. The Lookouts provide a fun-filled atmosphere with promotions, activities between innings and stunning views of the surrounding mountains.

SOCCER'S GROWING PRESENCE: NASHVILLE SC

Soccer fans shouldn't miss Nashville SC, the city's Major League Soccer team, which plays at the new Geodis Park. Soccer has rapidly grown in popularity in Tennessee, and Nashville SC's games showcase the sport's thrilling pace and the city's enthusiastic support for its newest team. The stadium creates an electrifying atmosphere that reflects soccer's rising status in the heart of Tennessee.

TIPS FOR SPORTS FANS

When attending sports events in Tennessee:

- Buy tickets in advance, especially for high-demand games like NFL, NBA or major college football matchups.
- Dress in team colors to enhance the experience and connect with local fans.
- Arrive early to enjoy pre-game festivities like tailgating, and to navigate parking and stadium entry.
- Check the stadium policies on items like bags and cameras to ensure a smooth entry.

23

LEARN TO SPEAK TENNESSEAN

Welcome to the heart of the Volunteer State, where the Southern drawl harmonizes with the rolling hills, and the language is as warm and inviting as a front porch swing on a summer evening.

In this chapter, we invite you to take a delightful journey through the charming and colorful world of Tennessean speech. From familiar Southern expressions to distinctive local terms, you'll explore the phrases that paint a vivid picture of life in this vibrant state. Whether you're a native Tennessean or a visitor eager to decipher the local lingo, these words and sayings will help you embrace the essence of Tennessee's culture and community, from "bless your heart" to "fixins," and beyond.

While some of these terms might also be heard in other parts of the American South, they all contribute to the rich tapestry of Southern vernacular that makes speaking Tennessean a true delight.

BACK FORTY
A term for a remote or distant area of a property or land. "I'm headin' out to the back forty to check on the cows." It refers to 40 acres, which were originally $1/4^{th}$ of an acreage laid out for farmers during the Homestead Act.

BBQ
In the South, the term BBQ is referring to the food, not the event. A cookout is where you gather as friends and family and eat BBQ. BBQ in this context is a slow-cooked meat, usually pork or beef. "I'm bringing my famous BBQ pulled pork to the family reunion this year—it's always a hit with everyone."

BLESS YOUR HEART / BLESS THEIR HEART
It's a way of expressing sympathy or empathy for someone's unfortunate situation or behavior, while also subtly acknowledging their shortcomings or difficulties. Basically, it's like a warm hug wrapped in a backhanded compliment. So, when you hear a Southerner say "Bless their heart," just know it's code for "They're trying, but Lord help 'em!"

BUGGY
Instead of "shopping cart" or "trolley," you might hear people refer to it as a "buggy" when grocery shopping. "Can you grab a buggy on your way in?"

BUGGY WHIP
A playful term used to describe a very old or outdated item or idea. "That old computer is about as useful as a buggy whip."

CATTYWAMPUS
A term used to describe something that is skewed, crooked or not aligned correctly. "The picture frame is all cattywampus."

COKE
In some parts of Tennessee, people refer to all soft drinks as "Coke" regardless of the brand. For example, "I'll have a Coke" might mean any carbonated soft drink.

COME HELL OR HIGH WATER
An expression used to emphasize determination or commitment. "I'll be there, come hell or high water."

COOKOUT
An outdoor gathering of friends and family where you eat BBQ and other fixins, such as coleslaw, baked beans, cornbread, corn-on-the-cob and potato salad. "We're having a cookout this Saturday to celebrate Dad's birthday, so don't forget to bring your appetite!"

CORNPONE
A type of cornbread made from simple ingredients like cornmeal, water and salt, often cooked in a skillet. "Pass me a piece of that cornpone."

COTTON-PICKIN'
An exclamation of frustration or irritation. "This cotton-pickin' traffic is drivin' me nuts!"

DADGUM
A mild exclamation used to express frustration or annoyance. "Dadgum it, I locked my keys in the car again!"

DERN TOOTIN'
An emphatic way to agree with someone or express strong affirmation. "You betcha, that's dern tootin'!"

FARSEE
A unit of measurement for distances. It's a shortened way of saying "far as you can see," as in "Y'all, we're gonna need to walk a farsee to get to the fishing spot down by the creek."

FISH FRY
A social gathering or event where fish is fried and served as the main dish. Usually, the fish used is freshwater fish like the catfish, crappie, bass or bluegill. "We're fixin' to have ourselves a proper fish fry down by the river this weekend. Got plenty of catfish and hushpuppies to go around—y'all better come hungry!"

FIXINS
Refers to side dishes or accompaniments to a meal. "We've got fried chicken with all the fixins for dinner."

FIXIN' TO OR FIXINTO
This phrase is often said as one word and means getting ready to do something. "I'm fixin' to head down to the store."

GRINNIN' LIKE A POSSUM EATN' A SWEET TATER
An expression used to describe someone with a big, happy grin or smile.

GRITS
A Southern dish made from ground corn, often served as a side dish with breakfast. "I'll have eggs and grits, please."

HITCHIN' POST
A place where you tie up your horse, or used humorously to refer to where you park your car. "I'll meet you at the hitchin' post."

HOLLER
A small, narrow valley between mountains, and also used to describe shouting or calling out loudly. "I heard him hollerin' from the holler."

HUSHPUPPIES
A popular side dish made from a mixture of cornmeal, flour, eggs, milk or buttermilk, baking powder and seasonings. The batter is shaped into small balls or elongated shapes and then deep-fried until golden brown and crunchy. Hushpuppies are often served with BBQ, fried fish or other seafood dishes, and generally accompanied with a dipping sauce.

LOOKEE HERE
A way to call attention to something noteworthy or surprising and another way of saying, "look at this," or "look here." "Hey, lookee here! Billy just caught the biggest catfish I've ever seen."

LIGHTNIN' BUG
Another name for a firefly, which are commonly found in Tennessee. "Back porch sittin', sweet tea sippin', and watchin' them lightnin' bugs flicker in the summer twilight—that's the Tennessee way."

MASH
To press or push, often used when talking about pushing a button or key on a remote or keyboard. "Could you mash that button to call the elevator?"

MAW AND PAW
Affectionate terms for one's parents, often used in rural settings. "Maw and Paw are comin' over for supper."

ME-MAW
"Me-Maw" is a term used in Tennessee and the broader Southern region to affectionately refer to one's grandmother, often on the maternal side of the family. "I spent the weekend at Me-Maw's house, and she taught me how to make her famous peach cobbler."

MUDDY THE WATERS
To create confusion or complicate a situation. "Don't muddy the waters; we need a clear plan."

ONCED
Another way to say "one time" or "once." "I onced tried to make Me-Maw's famous peach cobbler, and let me tell you, it was a disaster!'

TWICED
Where onced is once, twiced means "two times." "I've twiced been to the Great Smoky Mountains, and I'm already planning my next trip back!"

OVER YONDER
A directional term meaning a short distance away but not precisely specified. "The store's just over yonder."

PIDDLIN'
Doing something in a slow, leisurely manner. "I spent the afternoon piddlin' around in the garden."

PA-PAW
"Pa-Paw" (or "Paw-Paw") is a term used in Tennessee and the broader Southern region to affectionately refer to one's grandfather, typically on the paternal side of the family. "I always loved spending summers with Pa-Paw; he taught me how to fish and shared stories about the good ol' days."

POKE
A paper bag, often used when referring to a small bag of groceries. "I picked up a poke of groceries at the store."

SUPPER
Another term for the evening meal or dinner. Supper often consists of Southern comfort foods like fried chicken, mashed potatoes, collard greens, cornbread and sweet tea. "C'mon over y'all, Mama's fixin' up a big ol' supper with fried catfish, hushpuppies and all the fixins'".

SWEATIN' LIKE A SINNER IN CHURCH
A humorous way to describe someone who is sweating profusely due to hot weather or nervousness.

TOBOGGEN
Another word for a knit hat or beanie, typically worn to keep the head warm in cold weather. This can cause some confusion for those not from the Southern USA, since the more common definition of the term "toboggan" is a sled used for sliding on snow. "When winter comes around, don't forget to grab your toboggan to stay warm while working outside."

TATER
Short for potato, often used in phrases like "tater salad" or "mashed taters." "Pass me the fried taters."

TOO BIG FOR HIS BRITCHES

An expression describing someone who is acting overly confident or arrogant, often beyond their actual abilities or status. "Ever since he got that promotion, he's been acting too big for his britches—like he owns the whole company!"

Y'ALL

A condensed way to say "You All," and can refer to anywhere from one to many people. "Y'all coming to the cookout for the BBQ this weekend? We're gonna have a blast!"

ALL YA'LL

Another way to say "Ya'll," but it's usually said to a larger group of people. "I told all y'all to be here by noon, and look, half of y'all are still missing."

WALMARTIN OR WALLY WORLD

Walmartin is used as a verb and Wally World is a playful nickname for "Walmart." "We're just Walmartin' this afternoon to pick up some groceries and check out the deals at Wally World."

WHIPPERSNAPPER

A playful term used to describe a young, energetic person, often with a hint of affectionate teasing. "Look at that little whippersnapper run!"

24

ODD TENNESSEAN LAWS

NO SKUNKS ALLOWED… AS PETS
Tennessee does indeed prohibit the ownership of skunks as pets. The law is likely in place due to concerns about rabies and the potential for skunks to carry the disease.

NO USING X-RAYS FOR SHOE FITTINGS
Believe it or not, it used to be common for shoe stores to use X-ray machines to measure customers' feet for proper shoe fitting. However, Tennessee, like many other states, eventually banned this practice due to concerns about radiation exposure.

NO BEAR WRESTLING MATCHES
In Tennessee, it's illegal to participate in or promote bear wrestling matches. While this might seem like common sense, the fact that it had to be explicitly banned suggests that it was once a real concern!

NO SELLING MORE THAN TWO CARS PER YEAR WITHOUT A DEALER'S LICENSE
In Tennessee, it's illegal to sell more than two cars per year without a dealer's license. This law aims to regulate the sale of vehicles and prevent unlicensed individuals from engaging in large-scale car sales.

ADULTERY AND FORNICATION ARE ILLEGAL
It's still technically illegal to commit adultery in Tennessee. The law is not enforced but remains on the books.

FORTUNE TELLING
Telling someone's fortune or practicing "occult psychic powers" is forbidden in some parts of Tennessee.

SNAKE HANDLING
In Tennessee, it's legal to handle snakes for religious reasons, but there are rules you have to follow. This practice is mostly seen in certain Pentecostal churches, where people believe that handling venomous snakes shows their trust in God's protection. Even though it's allowed by law, there are safety regulations in place. You need permits and have to follow safety rules to make sure nobody gets hurt.

NOODLING IS LEGAL IN TENNESSEE
Noodling, also known as hand fishing, is a traditional method of catching catfish using only the hands. Popular in states like Tennessee, Mississippi and Oklahoma, noodlers locate catfish hiding in underwater cavities, such as hollow logs or riverbank holes, by feeling around with their hands. Once a fish is located, noodlers swiftly grab it by the mouth or gills and bring it to the surface. While exhilarating, noodling can be risky due

to encounters with other aquatic creatures like snapping turtles, snakes, beavers and even alligators.

While legal, there are some regulations in place. These regulations include restrictions on the size or species of fish that can be caught using this method, as well as requirements for fishing licenses or permits.

ILLEGAL TO HUNT WHALES IN TENNESSEE
It is illegal to hunt whales in Tennessee, even though the state is landlocked and there are no whales in the state's waters. While it might seem unnecessary given the geographical context, such laws are part of broader conservation and animal protection measures.

QUOTABLES & QUIRKY TENNESSEE-ISMS

Quotes

"Nashville is wicked. It's like a proper music community, but it's also quintessentially American. You bump into people there with cowboy hats that spit in jars and call you 'boy.' I just love that."

– ED SHEERAN, SINGER-SONGWRITER

"Tennessee: Where the mountains touch the sky and the music touches the soul."

– UNKNOWN

"I belonged to Nashville before I belonged to anyone."

– BRANDI CARLILE, SINGER-SONGWRITER

"The thing you can count on in life is that Tennessee will always be scorching hot in August."

– ANN PATCHETT, AUTHOR

"Tennessee: Where the music flows like the rivers and the people dance to their own beat."

– UNKNOWN

"We are famous for our three grand divisions of East, Middle and West Tennessee, represented by the three stars on our flag. It is important however to remember that the blue circle around the three stars on our flag represents the unity of our state. I believe that Tennesseans have much more that unites us than divides us."

– BILL LEE, TENNESSEE'S 50TH GOVERNOR

Official & Popular State Slogans

"Tennessee: America at its Best" - Popular State Slogan that was officially adopted as the state slogan in 1965 and is widely used to describe the pride and unique qualities of Tennessee.

"The Stage is Set for You" - This slogan emphasizes Tennessee's vibrant arts and music scenes, inviting visitors to enjoy and participate in its cultural offerings.

"Sounds Good to Me" - Used to highlight Tennessee's rich musical heritage, particularly in cities like Nashville and Memphis, known for country, blues and rock 'n roll music.

"Follow Me to Tennessee" - This slogan is an invitation to explore the diverse attractions the state has to offer, from the Great Smoky Mountains to the lively streets of its cities.

Bumper Stickers Loved by Locals & Visitors

"Only Tenn-I-See" - A playful phrase often used on souvenirs, playing on the state's name to suggest that in matters of beauty or preference, Tennessee is the only state worth "seeing."

"I Brake for Country Music" - A fun sticker often seen on vehicles in and around Nashville, the heart of country music.

Tennessee - It's Knot Just for Country" - A pun on the state's musical reputation and the word 'not,' suggesting there's much more to Tennessee than country music.

"Let's Get Rocky Topped!" - A spirited shout-out to the University of Tennessee fans and the state's mountainous terrains.

"I'm in a State of Tennessee" - A play on words indicating a blissful or content state of being, as well as being physically present in the state.

"Grin and Bear It in the Smokies" - A humorous take on experiencing the Smoky Mountains, home to the black bear.

"It's All About the Bass, No Treble - Tennessee Fishing" - For the fishing enthusiasts, a nod to catching bass in Tennessee's rivers.

"Nash-vegas, Baby!" - A fun reference to Nashville's lively entertainment scene, drawing a parallel with Las Vegas.

In Tennessee, we...

In Tennessee, we…
"…take our barbecue seriously, and a 'little friendly competition' means a day-long cook-off with secret family recipes."

In Tennessee, we…
"…don't need a watch to tell it's summer; the chorus of cicadas singing in the trees is timekeeper enough."

In Tennessee, we…
"…consider gravy a beverage and biscuits a utensil."

In Tennessee, we…
"…say 'it's not the heat, it's the humidity' and mean it, especially when it feels like walking through a warm bath."

In Tennessee, we…
"…know that 'bless your heart' can be a term of endearment or a polite Southern scolding."

In Tennessee, we…
"…understand that a front porch is more than a construction feature—it's a way of life."

In Tennessee, we…
"…are as passionate about our whiskey as we are about our religion, and in some parts, they're one and the same."

In Tennessee, we…
"…might forget your name but we'll remember how you like your tea: sweet."

In Tennessee, we…
"…don't get surprised by a random 'yee-haw!'—it's just another way to express joy or approval."

In Tennessee, we…
"…dance to the music of a fiddle as easily as we do to a rock guitar solo."

In Tennessee, we…
"…treat strangers like neighbors and neighbors like family."

In Tennessee, we…
"…pride ourselves on hospitality so much that saying 'no' to seconds is almost an insult."

QUIZ YOURSELF

1. How many official state songs does Tennessee have?

    A. One
    B. Three
    C. Ten
    D. Twelve

2. What is the capital of Tennessee?

    A. Memphis
    B. Nashville
    C. Knoxville
    D. Chattanooga

3. Which historic music venue is located in Nashville and is considered the "Mother Church of Country Music"?

   A. Ryman Auditorium
   B. The Grand Ole Opry
   C. Tootsie's Orchid Lounge
   D. Bluebird Cafe

4. What is the state nickname of Tennessee?

   A. The BBQ State
   B. The Sunshine State
   C. The Friendly State
   D. The Volunteer State

5. Which national park, straddling the border between North Carolina and Tennessee, is the most visited national park in the United States?

   A. Blue Ridge Parkway
   B. Great Smoky Mountains National Park
   C. Yosemite National Park
   D. Yellowstone National Park

6. What famous Jack Daniel's product is made in Lynchburg, Tennessee?

   A. Bourbon
   B. Scotch
   C. Tennessee Whiskey
   D. Rye Whiskey

7. Which popular soft drink was invented in Tennessee?

    A. Coca-Cola
    B. Dr. Pepper
    C. Pepsi
    D. Mountain Dew

8. Which major river forms the western border of Tennessee?

    A. Tennessee River
    B. Ohio River
    C. Missouri River
    D. Mississippi River

9. Which state does NOT border Tennessee?

    A. North Carolina
    B. West Virginia
    C. Mississippi
    D. Alabama

10. Tennessee is tied with Missouri as being the state bordered by the most states with eight.

    A. True
    B. False

11. The Parthenon in Nashville is an exact replica of the original Parthenon in Athens, Greece.

    A. True
    B. False

12. The official state sport of Tennessee is Stock Car Racing.

   A. True
   B. False

13. Tennessee has two different time zones.

   A. True
   B. False

14. The Smoky Mountains get their name from the smoke that used to rise from ancient campfires in the area.

   A. True
   B. False

15. Both Grizzly and black bears live in Tennessee.

   A. True
   B. False

16. The famous Jack Daniel's Distillery is located in a dry county where the sale of alcohol is prohibited.

   A. True
   B. False

17. There is no entrance fee to the Great Smoky Mountain National Park.

   A. True
   B. False

18. The official state fruit of Tennessee is the gooseberry.

   A. True
   B. False

19. Elvis Presley's former home, Graceland, is the most visited home in the U.S., after the White House.

   A. True
   B. False

20. The tallest building in Tennessee is the AT&T Building in Nashville, also known as the "Batman Building."

   A. True
   B. False

QUIZ ANSWERS

1. How many official state songs does Tennessee have?

    A. One
    B. Three
    C. Ten
    D. Twelve

2. What is the capital of Tennessee?

    A. Memphis
    B. Nashville
    C. Knoxville
    D. Chattanooga

3. Which historic music venue is located in Nashville and is considered the "Mother Church of Country Music"?

   A. Ryman Auditorium
   B. The Grand Ole Opry
   C. Tootsie's Orchid Lounge
   D. Bluebird Cafe

4. What is the state nickname of Tennessee?

   A. The BBQ State
   B. The Sunshine State
   C. The Friendly State
   D. The Volunteer State

5. Which national park, straddling the border between North Carolina and Tennessee, is the most visited national park in the United States?

   A. Blue Ridge Parkway
   B. Great Smoky Mountains National Park
   C. Yosemite National Park
   D. Yellowstone National Park

6. What famous Jack Daniel's product is made in Lynchburg, Tennessee?

   A. Bourbon
   B. Scotch
   C. Tennessee Whiskey
   D. Rye Whiskey

7. Which popular soft drink was invented in Tennessee?

    A. Coca-Cola
    B. Dr. Pepper
    C. Pepsi
    D. Mountain Dew

8. Which major river forms the western border of Tennessee?

    A. Tennessee River
    B. Ohio River
    C. Missouri River
    D. Mississippi River

9. Which state does NOT border Tennessee?

    A. North Carolina
    B. West Virginia
    C. Mississippi
    D. Alabama

10. Tennessee is tied with Missouri as being the state bordered by the most states with eight.

    A. True
    B. False

11. The Parthenon in Nashville is an exact replica of the original Parthenon in Athens, Greece.

    A. True
    B. False

QUIZ ANSWERS

12. The official state sport of Tennessee is Stock Car Racing.

    A. True
    B. False (Tennessee doesn't have an official state sport)

13. Tennessee has two different time zones.

    A. True
    B. False

14. The Smoky Mountains get their name from the smoke that used to rise from ancient campfires in the area.

    A. True
    B. False (It's from natural fog that often hangs over the range, creating a mystical, smoke-like appearance.)

15. Both Grizzly and black bears live in Tennessee.

    A. True
    B. False

16. The famous Jack Daniel's Distillery is located in a dry county where the sale of alcohol is prohibited.

    A. True
    B. False

17. There is no entrance fee to the Great Smoky Mountain National Park.

   A. True
   B. False

18. The official state fruit of Tennessee is the gooseberry.

   A. True
   B. False (It's the tomato)

19. Elvis Presley's former home, Graceland, is the most visited home in the U.S., after the White House.

   A. True
   B. False

20. The tallest building in Tennessee is the AT&T Building in Nashville, also known as the "Batman Building."

   A. True
   B. False

ACKNOWLEDGMENTS

Creating this Tennessee fun fact book has been a fantastic journey, made possible by the incredible support and enthusiasm of so many wonderful people.

To my **editor, Joe Levit**—thank you for your sharp eye, valuable feedback, and encouragement throughout this process. I'm also grateful to my **fact checker, Hank Musolf**, whose dedication ensured every detail was accurate and that each page celebrates Tennessee's rich history and culture. To my **cover designer**, **Paul Hawkins,** thank you for crafting a cover that embodies the warmth and charm of Tennessee.

A heartfelt thank you to my wife, who took on the dual role of **second editor and master proofreader**. Your care and patience added the perfect polish to this book, and I couldn't have done it without you.

To my **beta readers**, especially William Harang, Loretta Crow, and Laura Horton, your enthusiasm and feedback brought this book a fresh perspective, making it better than I could have imagined. Your feedback shaped this book into something truly special.

I am also deeply grateful to those who allowed me to use their photos to bring these facts to life. Your generosity has added an incredible visual dimension to the book, helping readers connect even more with each fact.

Finally, to every reader who shares a love for Tennessee, I hope this book brings you as much joy as I had putting it together. Thank you for being a part of this journey!

DON'T FORGET YOUR FREE SPECIAL BONUS

As a **special bonus** and as a **thank you** for downloading this book, I created a **FREE companion quiz e-book** with **over 100 fun questions and answers** taken from this book.

Get the FREE bonus quiz e-book here:
https://tinyurl.com/tennessee-bonus

Test your knowledge of Tennessee and quiz your friends. Enjoy!

LEARN SOMETHING? PLEASE LEAVE A REVIEW

If you enjoyed this book, please share your thoughts in a REVIEW. Your sincere feedback is really helpful and I would love to hear from you!

Please leave a quick review on
Amazon at
https://tinyurl.com/tennessee-book-review

If Goodreads is more your thing, please share it there.
www.goodreads.com

Thank you so very much!

WANT TO BE A BETA READER?

Curious about getting an early look at my new fun fact books?

Beta readers are the awesome folks who read early drafts before they hit the shelves, sharing feedback and helping make each chapter the best it can be.

Click on the link below or scan the QR code

to sign up as a future beta reader.

https://tinyurl.com/KNB-beta-reader

I'm excited to have you along for the ride!

ABOUT THE AUTHOR

Marianne Jennings is a self-proclaimed adventure craver and an adventure addict. She proudly holds the title of favorite aunt to her eleven nieces and nephews, and is a lover of new foods and new experiences.

She loves facts and trivia like Tennesseans love their hot chicken and country music. To help introduce other places, people, and cultures to others, she likes to share interesting and fun facts that are entertaining and memorable.

If you'd like to learn more or join her mailing list, you can connect with Marianne at https://knowledgenuggetbooks.com or on Instagram.

instagram.com/knowledgenuggetbooks

ALSO BY MARIANNE JENNINGS

Entire Knowledge Nugget Book fun fact collection

So You Think You Know CANADA, Eh? (2nd Edition)

Amazing Tennessee!

Amazing Alaska!

Everything About Astronauts Vol 1 & 2

Quirky Careers & Offbeat Occupations

Christmas Fun Facts!

www.ingramcontent.com/pod-product-compliance
Lightning Source LLC
Chambersburg PA
CBHW070616030426
42337CB00020B/3818